SOVIET-EAST EUROPEAN DIALOGUE
International Relations of a New Type?

SOVIET-EAST EUROPEAN DIALOGUE
International Relations of a New Type?

Nish Jamgotch, Jr.

The Hoover Institution
on War, Revolution and Peace
Stanford University • 1968

ACKNOWLEDGMENTS

Among those deserving special appreciation and gratitude are the Hoover Institution on War, Revolution and Peace, Stanford University, for its research grant and the use of its excellent library facilities during the summer of 1966; the Russian Research Center, Harvard University, for its appointment of me as Associate and the use of its facilities in the summer of 1967; and the Foundation, University of North Carolina at Charlotte, for its financial support toward the completion of the manuscript.

A number of professional colleagues shared their thoughtful views on the more questionable arguments and controversial ideas of this monograph. I am grateful to all whose constructive observations and encouragement undoubtedly benefited the final product. Needless to say, the responsibility for both values and shortcomings is mine alone.

N. J.

Cambridge, Mass.
June 1967

CONTENTS

SOVIET-EAST EUROPEAN DIALOGUE

INTRODUCTION

Political reverberations in the Communist world (called,
in this study, the international socialist system) continue to
highlight more than ever the relationships between the USSR
and the Marxist-Leninist states of Eastern Europe. Through
their participation in the Council for Mutual Economic Cooperation (COMECON) and the Warsaw Pact, these states
collectively constitute a unique international subsystem with
a vested interest, identity, and unifying mission of its own.
As the Soviet leadership is increasingly pressed to rely upon
the support of its closest allies in the conflict with China,
the seven members of this subsystem jointly experience the
most important single test of whether the communism projected by Soviet ideologies is to be the "wave of the future"
or not. Especially pertinent is the question of whether
Marxism-Leninism is genuinely appropriate to the requirements of a rapidly evolving international community, or
whether it merely bears a somewhat restricted utility as
ideological motivation for less developed states in the throes
of hectic modernization. More than this, the Soviets are
defending a crucial Marxist-Leninist social experiment, the
success or failure of which will have profound consequences

11

for communism as a potentially international achievement and even for continued one-party rule in the USSR itself.

There is no denying that in many Communist capitals, compelling reappraisals have been made in the face of intra-system altercation and continuous exposure to international problems beyond the pale of Marxist-Leninist solutions. Similarly, the West has revised its views: while some observers continue to affirm that the USSR is conspiratorially and routinely fulfilling every prophesy of Marx and Lenin, the overwhelming majority of Western specialists in international relations sees as the most extraordinary impact of contemporary Communist politics its very failure to achieve doctrinaire objectives—and what is more, they see no genuine prospect that these goals will ever be achieved as envisioned.

After more than a decade of polycentric communism, it is especially appropriate to examine the resultant policy changes and their portent for the internationalist goals of the USSR. The intention is to concentrate not so much on past or potential Soviet military aggression in Eastern Europe, as upon the more intellectually demanding questions of why the USSR has insisted upon influencing the politics of its East European neighbors, and what kind of policies it is presently pursuing in this sensitive area of traditional national interest.

The idea that the Soviets are militarily expansionist and ideologically motivated by an immutable desire to sovietize the world has long tended to produce distorted notions of their far more limited aims and objectives in areas of the world where subtle strategies and tactics are utilized, often with considerable success. And so it is with Eastern Europe

12

where the record of the Kremlin's foreign policy bears a number of clues for understanding the _multiple_ imperatives of Soviet political behavior. The first of these imperatives, traditional and by no means restricted to the USSR, has been the defense of areas deemed vital to territorial security. The second concerns the ideological mission of a vast and powerful nation which has assumed a solemn responsibility to promote a boldly utopian social experiment which may be cited as proof that Marx and Lenin were correct and that this may well be the Soviet century after all. Posing as the chief guardian of proletarian revolution in its contemporary setting—which is to say a frustrating and disappointing preoccupation with waning proofs—the Soviets have persevered to ease the transformation of international communism and sustain their primacy through a number of enterprises presumably reflecting international relations of a new type. The practical and theoretical aspects of these new relations warrant close analysis—a project which forms a special part of this study.

Yet a third imperative of Soviet behavior is the need to defend the political institutions of "socialism in one country" which at first were oppressive and harsh, and then much less so as the Communist Party elite took measures to refine and sophisticate state controls and rationalize the processes of industrialization. Not surprisingly, burgeoning vested interests and conservatism in Soviet society, plus a longing on the part of the populace to enjoy the benefits of civilized life now, have sapped the Party's doctrinaire goals and vitality. It must not be forgotten that the continued legitimacy of the Communist Party of the Soviet Union cannot simply be taken for granted as the revolutionary situation for which it was devised recedes into historical memory. Constant sources of both renewed and novel authority must be supplied.

At the outset of any inquiry into Soviet-East European relations, it is well to bear in mind that even fifty years after the Bolshevik Revolution the official scholarly view of the Soviet Union's revolutionary mission is by no means a modest one:

> The building of Communism in the USSR is mankind's greatest accomplishment in the whole of its history. Each new step which brings the Soviet Union nearer to Communism inspires the working people of all countries and provides tremendous moral support for all peoples struggling for the liberation from social and national oppression. "It is . . . by the example of a more perfect organization of society, by rapid progress in developing the productive forces, the creation of all conditions for the happiness and well-being of man, that the ideas of Communism win the hearts and minds of the masses," the Program of the CPSU points out.
>
> The Soviet people are entrusted with the mission of trail-blazers to mankind's radiant future. The experience of the CPSU and the Soviet state serves as a model for all the peoples fighting for Socialism and Communism.
>
> For nearly half a century the Soviet Union has been consistently applying the Leninist

14

> foreign policy of peace and friendship among
> nations. This policy has yielded priceless
> fruits. The success of Socialist and Com-
> munist construction in the USSR irrefutably
> proves its correctness. [1]

The irresistible questions are: to what extent do these ideological expressions of faith maintain the Soviet Union's predominance in systemwide Communist affairs? What is their augury for the worldwide movement as a whole? And what factors in turn have caused the Soviets to pursue their interests in Eastern Europe so tenaciously—at times even violently—and then to modify their behavior through highly flexible approaches toward ideological and organizational unity? The following study cannot give quantitative replies to any of these questions, but it can hopefully indicate some directions in which answers may be found.

Here, then, is first an addition to the rapidly accumulating literature advocating a reevaluation of ingrained and almost conditioned American responses to what the Soviets accomplished for themselves in the immediate postwar period; and second, an attempt to offer some fresh analytical perspectives on a number of contemporary, theoretical and practical relationships between Eastern Europe and the Soviet Union. Five topics receive primary consideration: (1) the international socialist system; (2) its East European core; (3) communism—an international doctrine; (4) the role of East European international organizations; and (5) Soviet international relations of a new type.

Especially difficult in researching a highly dynamic field is the problem of determining a cutoff date. The scope of this study is restricted in the main to the decade ending in the early fall of 1966, although subsequent events have tended to bear out the major judgments of that decade.

THE INTERNATIONAL SOCIALIST SYSTEM[1]

The slogan appearing daily on the front page of Pravda, "Proletarians of All Countries Unite," testifies to the Soviet goal of world proletarian unity, and communism is in its aspirations and projections potentially universal. For the present, however, the rubric, "international system," comes closest to reflecting accurately the rather wide scope and organizational variety of communism within clearly definable areas of the world. Since it is within an environment of fourteen ruling-party states that the most significant Soviet-East European relations are conducted, a brief analysis of the structure and dynamics of the international socialist system as a whole should prove useful.

The key to the functioning of the current arrangement is to be found in the existence of two giant powers of comparable rank—one more powerful for the present, the other less but possibly in the long run the stronger of the two. During China's civil war and reconstruction, the Soviet Union was communism's sole great-power advocate and defender, and Stalin was easily able to exert an unchallenged leadership which long served to obscure portentous transformations in the locus and distribution of world power. After

Mao Tse-tung's victory on the Chinese mainland and the passing of Stalinism, an unexpected dimension appeared. Harboring the seeds of competition and conflict, a second Communist force emerged and extended itself until, in 1956-57, it succeeded in influencing Eastern Europe on behalf of greater national independence. Thus began the shift from the rigidity of a bloc to a truly operational bipolar system in which degrees of national diversity and independence became both legitimate and tenable.

It is, of course, possible to argue that such a situation had already come into being with Marshal Tito's successful defiance of the Kremlin in 1948 and the subsequent maintenance of Yugoslav independence in the face of a variety of Soviet pressures. Indeed, it would be wrong to minimize the motivational significance of the Yugoslav model and its singular impact in generating the initial impetus toward polycentric communism. For purposes of system operation, however, Yugoslav political power alone proved insufficient to effect a condition of true bipolarity. Chinese communism is not merely of a markedly different brand. It is supported by the kind of political and economic strength which can encourage fluid allegiance and varying international power configurations, thus providing multiple foreign policy options for minor Communist powers and initiating a whole new era in the future of the international movement as well.

Quite paradoxically, strained and disruptive Sino-Soviet relations have generated a number of consequences important to the system's health and well-being. The very existence of protracted great-power Communist conflict has provided safety valves for bold national self-assertion and political diversity, all of which renders international Marxism-Leninism more flexible and attractive to outsiders. Simultaneously, greater opportunities for political and economic integration within smaller and more homogeneous sectors, both East European and Asian, have arisen. The present international system is surely less cohesive than an alliance or a bloc, but for this very reason it possesses more internal resilience, and its individual units in turn gain the ability to resist unwanted pressures and blandishments. Most of all, being more plastic today than ever before, its potential for reciprocal accommodation and adaptation through a process of active intrasystem exchanges and interrelationships is substantially enhanced. The resultant activity preserves the political integrity of individual members, maintains a community of heterogeneous interests, reinforces a unique joint identity distinguishing the Marxist-Leninist camp from all other international groups—and at the same time demonstrates a collective separateness at variance with the notion of Marxist-Leninist universalism.

It is not too much to say that the development of polycentric communism has actually promoted informal conflict-management and conflict-containment in which a variety of confrontations, pitting one national authority against another, commonly take place. Basic agreement on avowed aims and aspirations still exists; but if there is a predominant message in the intrasystem politics of the post-Stalin years, it is that occasions for sharp conflict can arise among ruling-party states as assuredly as in other international systems. In short, the politics of the international socialist system is characterized by discernible alignments on both theoretical and policy-oriented issues. For example, major differences arise over the meaning and repercussions of "separate roads to socialism," the optimum scope and degree of Soviet tutelage in Communist affairs, the inevitability of war, the scope and substance of "peaceful coexistence," the problem of the transition to communism, and the specific forms of aid to bourgeois nationalist forces throughout the underdeveloped parts of the world.

The maintenance of a monolithic power structure has long been considered essential to communism. Any tendency to polarize around two points of leadership has had to be avoided because of potentially grave dangers to the tenets and requirements of the Marxist-Leninist faith. Twice it has been necessary to convoke major international conferences of Party leaders from all quarters to head off the threat presented by super divisions within the Communist world. The first occasion, in 1957, followed Khrushchev's repudiation of the Stalinist cult and the suppression of the Hungarian Revolt. The second, in late 1960, bore largely upon the problems of militancy and ascendancy between the two principal centers of Communist power. The 1960 meeting centered on important differences regarding the prospects of an ultimate victory for communism while simultaneously minimizing the risks of thermo-nuclear war. The keynote of the conference

20

was an attitude of mutual flexibility and exchange expressed in a final communique issued in the name of world Communist leaders. One portion went as follows:

> All the Marxist-Leninist parties are independent and have equal rights, they shape their policies according to the specific conditions in their respective countries and in keeping with Marxist-Leninist principles, and they support one another. The success of the working-class cause in each country demands the internationalist solidarity of all Marxist-Leninist parties. Each party is responsible to the working-class, to the working people of its country, to the international working-class and Communist movement as a whole.
>
> The Communist and workers' parties hold meetings whenever necessary to discuss urgent problems, to exchange experience, acquaint themselves with each other's views and positions, work out common views through consultations and coordinate joint actions in the struggle for common goals.
>
> The experience and results of the meetings of representatives of the Communist Parties held in recent years, particularly the results of the two major meetings—that of November 1957, and this meeting—show that in present-day conditions, such meetings are an effective form of exchanging views and experience, enriching Marxist-Leninist theory by collective effort and elaborating uniform positions in the struggle for common objectives. [2]

Soviet efforts both before and after Khrushchev's forced retirement have been directed toward forging consensus through preparatory conferences in anticipation of a third all-inclusive gathering of the world's Communist parties. In March 1965, the Soviets belatedly attempted to promote some semblance of system unity and at the same time to float a trial balloon for mild disciplinary prodding of the Chinese—an effort which proved singularly unsuccessful. The statement which climaxed the consultative meeting of nineteen parties (twenty-six were invited) was pale in comparison with earlier testimonials supporting Soviet leadership. Coming somewhat as a letdown to residual pro-Soviet loyalties, the statement re-emphasized the "independence and equality of all fraternal parties" and suggested that an erosion of Soviet prestige had taken place. One need only recall that in 1957 the CPSU had been declared the "head" of the movement, with the concurrence of the Chinese themselves. At the 1960 gathering, the Soviet Party was still said to be the "universally recognized vanguard." But in the 1965 rally, even dominated as it was by distinctly pro-Soviet parties, no special paeans or precedence were accorded the Soviets, and the prevalent tone was one of frank admission that inter-party differences over serious problems of theory and practice existed.

Again, sessions at Karlovy Vary, Czechoslovakia (April 1967) were designed to prepare for a world conference on the 1 and 1960 models but without their shortcomings. Meeting to consolidate the progressive revolutionary forces of the world, this forum of European Communist and workers' parties proved more a striking demonstration of general proletarian internationalism than of socialist internationalism among the fourteen Marxist-Leninist states alone. Although Albania declined invitation, and the League of Communists of Yugoslavia and the Rumanians did not participate, major communiques served to emphasize the presence of Eastern Europe's ruling parties. The gathering was highlighted by its pronounced European (as opposed to systemwide) character and by the Soviet Union's own quite modest role and leadership. As to the real significance of that meeting, it may be far too early for conjecture; but the Karlovy Vary conference may well have marked the beginning of a series of regional European party gatherings which will serve to render a world conference unnecessary.

To highlight the most pressing problems of the present international socialist system, one needs to recall the specific ways in which Soviet leaders reacted to challenges and opportunities in the aftermath of World War II. The early tendency was to rivet Soviet controls upon nearby territories which had fallen under the influence of the Red Army. In the case of Eastern Europe, ultimate security meant the support of bogus coalition governments, followed by the establishment of completely subservient regimes in the form of transitional people's democracies. As we know, there was an eventual easement of tensions, together with the establishment of more flexible institutions for insuring cohesion. Although the 20th Party Congress (February 1956) supported the notion that national diversity was quite within the purview of Leninist orthodoxy, this did not mean that the USSR had intentionally fostered separate roads to socialism. Such roads were

byproducts of gradual evolution, a good part of it characterized by upheaval and violence. And despite reasonable expectations that Chairman Khrushchev's dispensation would
serve to preserve Soviet hegemonial interests over the regimes in Eastern Europe, neither the theoretical adjustment
to fact nor continued Soviet influence and military presence
guaranteed the continued subservience of these regimes either
Gradually, the absolutist relationships of the years immediate
following the war gave way to a more fluid pattern of contin-
gencies, with the USSR certainly occupying first place but
nevertheless displaying greater responsiveness to varying
and often conflicting nationalist aspirations of "fraternal
brothers." In brief, the history of Communist international
relations in the decade 1956-66 can be said to have consisted
in the main of continuous pragmatic adjustments on the part
of the Soviet Union to marked national independence and diversity among the East European states, followed by ideological heterogeneity clearly alien to the precepts of
Marxism-Leninism.

The serious liabilities in employing the tools of Marxism-
Leninism for the conduct of foreign policy were hardly apparent in Stalin's time. As long as the USSR was the only powerf
Communist state, Soviet political dispensations could be effec
tively challenged by none of the lesser associates except Yugo
slavia, which, because of its favored geographical position,
constituted a special case. However, with the eclipse of the
Soviet Union's power monopoly and self-declared infallibility
in dictating international proletarian causes, the avowed

universal applicability of Communist doctrine was irretriev-
ably blunted. There is little evidence that the Soviets ever
anticipated strong competition from an operational international system whose dynamics would pose serious risks to
ideological and political unity and, ultimately, to Soviet prestige itself. Their failure to assess accurately the vitality
of nationalist aspirations simply reflected a basic inadequacy
not only of Kremlin leadership, but also of fundamental
Marxist-Leninist categories, which provide no realistic approach to understanding the conflicting interests of discrete
national communities, even if those communities espouse common ideological goals.

At present, various national traditions throughout the
system are tenuously bridged by an action-oriented, futuristic ideology which argues that capitalism is doomed by the
processes of history and must inevitably be replaced by a
new social and political order of Communist derivation. Because of the presumed capitalist threat, like-minded parties
must maintain unity through fundamental similarities in policy.
Since policies are hardly enough, and because such unity cannot be maintained in the final analysis by force alone, a common ideological commitment becomes doubly vital. Communist
leaders must continue to sustain an indispensable commitment
to the future as the chief cohesive force uniting diverse nations
in various stages of evolution toward communism.

Divorced from a single coercive power center, Marxism-
Leninism has already been stretched to accommodate a variety of "revolutionary" experiences from the Elbe River to the

38th Parallel. Interpretations by national Communist elites have multiplied accordingly. The Soviet leadership for its part must increasingly anticipate the reactions of its international followers and make liberal allowances which may render the system more democratic to those who in the past have feared Soviet domination. This arrangement provides strength, assuming that controlled divisiveness does not lead to irreconcilable fractures or splits. But with an infallible ideological arbiter gone, every accommodation means that the formerly absolutist doctrine becomes progressively relative: the international socialist system as the embodiment of Soviet aspirations becomes visionary and open to substantial adjustments. And as the system comes closer to its goal of universality, there are greater possibilities for diversity and conflict among its increased number of adherents. One must question, for example, the relationship between doctrinal orthodoxy, precarious as this is already, and the importance of forward momentum—i. e. , the addition of new members. Here is the kind of conflict which further intensifies the problem of a unified ideological commitment, for it poses a serious question of whether the Kremlin can tailor foreign policies which can facilitate the prophesies of Marx and Lenin and yet preserve even a semblance of what they regarded as holy writ. Disintegrative tendencies might result in greater opportunities for security through legitimate power alignments within the system and, therefore, less need to rely upon rash independent action or even outside allies. But the attendant corrosive effects upon irreducible Marxist-Leninist foundations cannot but have a telling impact upon doctrinal orthodoxy as we know it.

Perhaps the greatest doubt for the future of the international socialist system lies in the contradiction between the monolithic organization of each Communist party demanding pervasive control over all important phases of a nation's political life, and the cardinal requisites of an international system—namely, independence, diversity, mutual responsiveness, and flexible organization. It should be obvious that mere multilateral or bilateral contacts negotiated among "equals," interpreting their own interests as the situation demands, do not supply those proper organizational instruments for international solidarity which Lenin consistently argued are essential for the triumph of world revolution. For the present, relationships within the system may reflect divergent unity with little palpable adverse effect; but at what point does divergence become so pronounced that even minimal unity is jeopardized? And what impact does this in turn have upon the Marxist-Leninist ideology which underpins the Communist approach to universalism, and, indeed, the Soviet and East European political processes themselves? In the past, Communists have found it difficult to operate in the style of traditional international relations, in which autonomous political systems are treated on an equal footing. Clearly the problems of ideological unity are enormous; but the incompatibility between the domestic experience of communism and the cross-pressures of contemporary international politics signifies further that great obstacles are yet to be confronted. The most crucial tests for the system may lie in its capacity to solve problems growing out of its increased exposure and hastening evolution within a pluralistic international environment.

This is not to say that Soviet decision-makers are unaware of these challenges, or that a tacit compromise solution has not been attempted, which, although far short of being either universal or system-wide, still bears meaning within the context of official expressions quoted earlier. The underlying thesis of this study is that even though the international socialist system technically includes all of the nation-states which have declared themselves in favor of Marxism-Leninism, the six states immediately west of the Soviet Union comprise by far its most significant collective component. The specific roles which Eastern Europe performs on behalf of Soviet interests are yet to be examined. For the moment it is well to reflect upon postwar Soviet-East European relations and bear in mind that simultaneously with the disintegration of a once monolithic bloc, the Soviet Union's attitude has become conspicuously more sensitive, rational, pragmatic, accommodating, and keenly receptive to developments suggesting ideological confirmation.

EASTERN EUROPE—CORE AND SUBSYSTEM[1]

A great deal of energy, in both official circles and academic communities, has long been expended in seeking the precise motives for Soviet policies in postwar Eastern Europe: Were they part of a Marxist-Leninist program to communize the world? Strategic moves to be expected from any great power in the wake of costly military victory? A result of Western diplomatic and military bungling, unwittingly consigning half of Europe to alien domination? No single answer is satisfactory, largely because enterprises dedicated to firm decisions on when the Soviets are Russians and when they are Communists are at best frustrating and elusive. The important truth for both Communist ideologists and the world is that the Soviet Union's hegemonistic posture in Eastern Europe confirmed not the predictions of Marx and Lenin, but rather the ability of the Red Army to push its way into a vast power vacuum caused by the War's devastation and the attendant collapse of Europe's Great Powers.

Whatever the precise motivation of the Soviets, the United States perceived their moves as essentially military challenges and countered with enormous quantities of economic and military aid to Western Europe. Although at the outset the relationship between Eastern Europe and the Soviet dedication to an international Communist society was neither clear nor certain, the Soviets soon reacted with their own organizational forms, culminating in 1955 in the Warsaw Pact which bound its signatories to a commitment that an attack upon one would be considered an attack upon all. There followed several highly significant indicators of Soviet policy trends, including repeated pronouncements favoring first collective economic growth, then promoting international equalization, and finally proposing a simultaneous entry into communism by fraternal Marxist-Leninist states "within one and the same historical epoch."[2] Once the USSR laced its satellites together in a military alliance, proved its reliability in exercising overwhelming punitive force during the Hungarian Rebellion in 1956, and, beginning in 1958, rejuvenated the Council for Mutual Economic Cooperation, the die was cast. In the Soviet purview, the territory of Eastern Europe had assumed a security priority comparable to that of the USSR itself.

Aside from the involvements of the Soviet Army in Hungary, an important downgrading of Eastern Europe's role in military strategy logically followed from the revolutionary developments in nuclear weaponry and the very nature of modern warfare. Stalin's original premonitions about the corridors through which foreigners traditionally marched to Russia, frequently expressed to both Roosevelt and Churchill during the wartime conferences and after, must be reexamined in the light of the present operational missile age, when either major competitor in the arms race is capable of annihilating the other regardless of who controls Eastern Europe. Official declarations from the Kremlin have also admitted that a decisive shift in the international balance of power has taken place in favor of the international socialist system.[3] Tracing their roots to Chairman Khrushchev's speech at the 20th Party Congress in 1956 and the launching of Sputnik in 1957, fresh Party views revealed that the danger of capitalist attack had apparently subsided to the point where the Chairman could state in a widely distributed tract in 1962 that the West would not risk a war against the socialist countries.[4] Thus, in addition to the reductive effect of the thermonuclear age, the original motives for Soviet controls in Eastern Europe have been modified by self-declared shifts in world power and by other developments mitigating the Soviet view of capitalist hostility.

But if it may be argued that in the missile age the western marches to the USSR no longer hold much strategic value, there is as yet no evidence that the Soviets regard the area as having less overall significance. There remains the question of why Eastern Europe persists as a high-priority security interest when it is likely that, in a deliberate war, attacks would be made directly upon home territory without the customary invasion probes from Central Europe. The point is that Eastern Europe embodies a new defense imperative inextricably tied to the political requirements of its powerful neighbor. The imperative stems not merely from continuing military strategies and tactics, however transformed by the impact of modern technology, but also from the crucial role in the enhancement of several interests bearing upon the continuation and fruition of the Soviet political system as we know it.

Thus, in an age when bombs may pass directly between nuclear adversaries and small intervening states tend to lose much of their importance as pawns or vantage points for war, the accretive nature of great-power interests may impart to such states a special <u>doctrinal</u> utility beyond the reach of purely military instruments. Of course, proximity to a powerful nation always poses for weaker states the traditional risk of engulfment. But the risks are of considerably more awesome magnitude when a great power's security interests must be continuously redefined and expanded in the name of a universalistic mission, even though its own territorial defense is assured. Once a power has committed itself to the worldwide application of its political doctrines, the preservation of its <u>regime</u> essence, as distinct from its territory, becomes a continuing responsibility and major concern. It is in this sense that the maintenance of Marxist-Leninist political systems of Eastern Europe has assumed added significance for the Soviet Union.

Within the context of multiple Soviet national interests, the grouping of the USSR, Poland, East Germany, Czechoslovakia, Hungary, Rumania, and Bulgaria may be profitably viewed as the core or central subsystem of a wider and analogous international configuration of fourteen members. Viewed in terms of four interrelated sectors in ascending order of priority, the USSR by virtue of its predominance and advancing Communist construction is the prime power and self-appointed guardian of the international <u>proletarian</u> movement (1), the leading power in its <u>more</u> developed segment, the international socialist system (2), the linchpin of its <u>most</u> progressive international sector—the East European subsystem (3), and finally, the preserver of its <u>own</u> national interest (4). The objective of the following three sections is to clarify more fully the multi-dimensional interdependence between sectors (3) and (4).

COMMUNISM—AN INTERNATIONAL DOCTRINE

In probing the theoretical foundations of Soviet rule, it is useful to bear in mind that, unlike the American political system, whose authority stems from various sources, none of them strictly defined, the Soviet leadership's governing mandate derives from its exclusive claim to be the sole repository and interpreter of Marxist-Leninist truth—i. e. , a single self-asserted source unquestioningly entitling the CPSU to a perpetual monopoly of political power. Central to this comparison is the distinction between a doctrine which is an integral part of a political culture but where rule is <u>also</u> legitimized through an electoral mechanism and ritual (US), and a philosophy the essential truth of which is <u>itself</u> deemed the sole legitimizing force (USSR).

The Soviet Union is governed by a party whose avowed ultimate function is to guide its people to communism—that is to say (even excluding matters of popular sovereignty, organized opposition, legitimate dissent, and rotation in office as proper forms of political expression), it is not a traditional political party in the Western sense. The CPSU must justify itself in the name of Marxism-Leninism, which is not a program for socialism in one country, but rather for

an infinitely more inclusive set of both quantitative and qualitative relationships at the international level. The thesis
that Marxism-Leninism is not a political ideology for national
development exclusively, but mature and genuine only in its
international and presumably final phase, establishes a unique
relationship between the USSR and those nations of the world
institutionally and ideologically committed to the same kind
of future. Officially stated, "The Soviet Union is not pursuing the tasks of communist construction alone but in fraternal
community with the other socialist countries."[1]

To the Soviets, the natural urge must be to maintain their
allegiance to internationalist goals, avoid radical revisions in
their political system, and at the same time defend, strengthen,
and perpetuate its dominant party, which has undergone continuous growth for fifty years and, according to its most recent Program, is not prepared to relinquish supremacy even
during the period of full-scale Communist construction. Although territorial security against foreign invasion is common-
place, regime security against unsettling transformations
which tend to belie doctrinal infallibility is a relatively new
phenomenon. It originates in the conviction that a select com-
posite of institutions and processes is an outgrowth of a political philosophy inevitably applicable to everyone. For this
reason, aside from economic and social values accruing
directly to Communist construction in the USSR, the "unflagging struggle abroad" bears momentous long-range security
implications. As authoritatively stated by International Affairs:

> Like the foreign policy of any state, Soviet
> foreign policy is a continuation of the coun-
> try's home policy.
>
> Clearly, the most favorable external con-
> ditions for building up Communism in our
> country will be secured when the ideals for
> which the Soviet people have fought and are
> fighting triumph in the rest of the world,
> i. e. , when Socialism and Communism are
> victorious all over the world.
>
> The viability of Soviet policy lies in the fact
> that this objective is practicable. The vital
> interests of the victorious Russian prole-
> tariat in its own country coincide with the
> mature requirements of world historical
> development, for Socialism and Communism
> embody the future of the entire planet. [2]

The Party's peculiar dilemma is at once revealed. Although national in scope, it must adhere with an unswerving
dedication to a doctrine which is claimed to be universally
applicable and inevitable of fulfillment. Committed in this
way, the CPSU must have it both ways: it must bear both
national and international responsibilities, and as long as it
arrogates to itself a revolutionary mission with both implicit
and explicit internationalist objectives, there is little choice
in the matter. As a consequence, its programs and the ideology behind them are tried in the dock of world opinion by
those who assay developments as either essential doctrinal
confirmation or a lack of it. To be sure, failure in such confirmation would not mean the demise of the Soviet regime or
its exclusive party. But the significant impairment of revolu-

tionary aspirations in the name of a mission with international scope would appear to be inescapable, unless of course fresh sources of political energy and legitimation are tapped.

As in every political system, the ruling elite of the CPSU must remain keen and attuned to the social changes which are shaping its course. The problem is especially acute for a maturing revolutionary regime for which justification and legitimacy cannot be provided forever by the dynamism of a bygone era. Increasingly challenging is the task of reconciling the aspirations of the Party elite, dedicated to maintaining its own monopoly and exclusiveness, with a rapidly advancing society craving a respite from the demands long imposed in the name of a revolutionary ideology. Already, the Soviet people are exhibiting the effects of the consumption ethic, and once a program of moderation has been launched—once the peoples of the USSR and Eastern Europe experience limited personal freedom and glimpse an image of abundance—the process is exceedingly difficult to reverse. Inclinations of the Soviet people toward political conservatism and complacency operate increasingly to render anachronistic many of the reasons for the organization and perpetuation of the CPSU in the first place, thus confirming the adage that the closer a revolutionary ideology comes to fulfillment, the greater the irrelevance of its instruments. The result has been a deep, erosive impact upon Marxist-Leninist ideology, further compounding (and compounded by) the problems caused by polycentrism at the international level, to which Party stalwarts must nonetheless constantly refer for guidance and legitimacy.

These unsettling complexities have affected the Soviet decision-making process itself. Although there appears to be agreement on ideological fundamentals within the Party's inner sanctum, this has not precluded serious reservations and differences over the formulation of concrete policy and the precise timing and speed of its implementation. Contrary to popular notions, recent research confirms that for a number of years, sharp differences have raged between militant and moderate groups over several issues, including, in addition to domestic questions, the international ramifications of public criticism of Stalin, the proper forms and degrees of accommodation with the West, the official stand to be taken toward the Chinese, support for Cuba, and so forth.[3] Extraordinary debates have ensued, reflecting serious concern over potentially abrupt transformations in the international socialist system and disruptive evolution in the Soviet political process as well. Such differences are an expression of a continuing need for groups in the domestic power structure to preserve the values and institutions which, in Lasswell's classic phrase, can continue to deliver deference, income, and safety—i. e. , the guarantees which provide not only the rewards of today, but also the promise of recognition and status in the future. This promise rests upon the ability of select elites to protect the Marxist-Leninist sources of their authority, perpetuate the system which delivers preferment, and at the same time modernize both, so as to fulfill the leadership's grandiose promises to the Soviet consumer.

By always relating its activities to basic doctrinal "truths," the CPSU has created for itself a boundless source of justification, continuity, and mission. But no social situation is static, and there is little reason to believe that doctrines which have long been persuasive and exciting can continue to be so. Much has changed since the frenetic months of 1917, and it is most unlikely that the Soviet regime can ever attain its self-proclaimed goals by depending upon a continuation of the precise forces that helped to create it. Indeed, after more than a generation, the early millenarian Communist faith has been profoundly modified by continuous confrontations with the persistent requirements of a modern public order system and the growing demands for economic and social advancement based upon empirical performance—not upon doctrinaire elocution or statistical deceptions. Ideologies, of course, bear inherent contradictions which reveal themselves as history unfolds; and the human mind, however predisposed, cannot in practice remain impervious to a penetrating feedback of reality. Doctrinaire social engineering, such as Stalin's breakneck five-year plans, totalitarian excesses, and irrational purges, has long since been abandoned; and already a host of changes in Soviet and East European economic life, plus unforeseen dissension within the Communist world, have obscured common ideals and led the system's observers to believe that a good part of Marxism-Leninism is erroneous.

This is not to say that if Marxist-Leninist ideology has lost some of its credibility and vitality, it has ceased to be important. Constant exhortations from official Communist

platforms betray a lasting penchant for legitimacy and a continuing need to perpetuate the notion of Marxist-Leninist
infallibility, ultimate Communist victory, and the Party's
indispensable role. Voluminous documentation appears in
the Soviet press, Kommunist, International Affairs, and the
World Marxist Review, reflecting unabashed optimism on the
part of Soviet spokesmen and the claim that the interdependence between the building of communism in the USSR and the
revolutionary process in other countries is positive only.
For example, the authoritative Fundamentals of Marxism-
Leninism provides the following interpretation of fraternal
mutual support as a new and specific element that distin-
guishes relations among socialist states:

> Socialism has the great advantage that it
> enables the national interests of each coun-
> try to be harmoniously combined with the
> interests of the world socialist system as a
> whole. Patriotism of the peoples of the
> socialist countries merges with interna-
> tionalism. Love for one's own socialist
> country is organically combined with love
> for the whole family of fraternal socialist
> nations. [4]

Or, as Pravda phrased it:

> We Communists may argue among ourselves.
> But . . . our firm principle and sacred duty
> is to educate the people of each country in a
> spirit of profound solidarity with all the peo-
> ples of the socialist commonwealth. We are
> obligated to inculcate in the people a love not
> only for their own country but for the other
> socialist countries as well, so that each person

40

will feel that he is a patriot both of his own country and of the entire world socialist commonwealth. [5]

How was such an environment, providing for dual loyalties, created?

> The Marxist-Leninists of the People's Democracies foresaw the possibility and historic necessity of overthrowing capitalist rule in their countries, of establishing the power of the working people . . . and carrying out the necessary socialist changes. Alive to these pressing needs of social development, they led the people along the path of building socialism, in which they have already achieved considerable success.

> Crucial developments in the first half of the century thus provide irrefutable proof that the Communists, armed with the Marxist theory, on the whole, correctly predicted the general course of history. The truth of the Marxist-Leninist conception of history has been fully borne out in practice. [6]

Referring to the interrelationship between world resolution and Soviet communism, Boris N. Ponomaryev, Secretary of the Party's Central Committee and Chairman of its International Department, wrote in November 1964:

> What is the interaction between the building of communism and the world revolutionary movement? Speaking in general terms, the building of communism in the USSR intensifies as a supreme manifestation of proletarian internationalism and the revolutionary movement throughout the world . . . . Building communism in the

USSR is a major part of the development
of the world revolutionary movement and
the struggle for the victory of socialism
throughout the world. On the other hand,
the unflagging struggle being waged by our
comrades abroad is of great help in the
building of communism in the USSR. The
revolutionary activity of Marxist-Leninists
of all countries weakens the imperialists'
forces, frustrates their subversive and
anti-Soviet designs, and contributes to the
spread of sympathy among working people
everywhere for the first country of socialism. [7]

Perhaps more incisively than any other contemporary

Western scholar, Richard Lowenthal as early as 1962 pro-

jected the grim reality and logic of such internationalist

commitments:

For the second time within five years, it
[the CPSU] will have to revise its image
of its own international role. In 1956,
Khrushchev ordered the party to abandon
the Stalinist concept that the progress of
world revolution was wholly dependent on
Soviet strength. Now it will have to unlearn
the Khrushchevian belief that the progress
of world revolution would invariably increase
that strength. Khrushchev was right in facing the fact that independent revolutions may
occur outside Soviet control; Stalin was right
in thinking that such revolutions may not
necessarily be to the advantage of the Soviet
Union. But if the progress of revolution and
the expansion of Soviet power are distinct
and sometimes mutually contradictory processes, it follows that the Soviet Union has
as little chance to win world hegemony as

42

any other power. This is not going to be
the Soviet Century after all. [8]

Understandably enough, Communist theoreticians have not
agreed with such critical forecasts. There is in their view
no ultimate incompatibility between proletarian internationalism and the requirements of any particular national interest;
and in the Communist world generally, the serious dangers
inhering in multiple interpretations of doctrinal orthodoxy
simply do not receive the widespread academic attention so
prevalent in the West. Todor Zhivkov, First Secretary of
the Bulgarian Communist Party, clarified the issue as follows:

> Let us repeat—such differences [national-
> ist divisiveness] are not historically in-
> evitable. They are inherent neither in the
> nature of the socialist system nor in the
> nature of the Communist parties. National-
> ism and other inimical trends will continue
> to exert pressure on the parties and to en-
> gender non-Marxist views. This is beyond
> doubt. But a normal Party life, a life un-
> affected by a personality cult and its con-
> sequences will be a powerful barrier in
> preventing these trends from penetrating
> deeply into the Party and influencing the
> political line of the socialist countries.
> The virus of nationalism will be with us
> for a long time. But to this the parties
> have a powerful antidote: loyalty to cre-
> ative Marxism-Leninism, Leninist adher-
> ence to principle, democratic centralism,
> criticism and self-criticism, and open con-
> flict of opinions. [9]

More recently, _Pravda_ offered a somewhat more sober
assessment:

> Throughout its long, arduous, but glori-
> ous and great, history, the world revolu-
> tionary movement has undergone many
> trials and overcome many difficulties.
> Each time it has emerged from these dif-
> ficulties still further strengthened and
> made wiser by experience. There can be
> no doubt that the present difficulties as
> well, borne of attempts to introduce dissen-
> tion in its ranks, will also be successfully
> overcome. A pledge of this is the vast ex-
> perience collectively accumulated by the
> fraternal parties and the steadfast will of
> all revolutionaries toward unity of action
> in the struggle against imperialism, for
> the great ideals of peace and socialism. 10

At the deep ideological level, nothing better illustrates
the telling refusal of Soviet leaders to face the disturbing realities of the international socialist system than these wishful
evasions. No serious exposure or analysis is made of the
potentially restrictive and negative consequences of the self-
declared interdependence between Communist construction in
the Soviet Union and social revolutions in distant parts of the
globe. No honest attempt is made to explicate the inescapable
facts of wide institutional diversity and increasingly tenuous
ideological unity—two developments largely due to the emergence of a formidable and errant China and various particularistic tendencies endemic to Eastern Europe. It is difficult
to avoid the conclusion that as long as the unmistakable trend
of the past decade continues, the realization of a single supranational proletarian interest will remain illusory, despite the
official statement that "love for one's own socialist country is

organically combined with love for the whole family of fraternal socialist nations." The allegedly scientific and infallible tenets of Marxism-Leninism notwithstanding, the notion that the goals of all workers of the world are synonymous or fully compatible with Soviet national interests has been and is likely to remain a doctrinal shibboleth.

Shibboleth or not, strains of fundamentalism are bound to persist, for as history has shown, universalistic doctrines die hard, and it is always difficult to exchange that which is familiar and consoling for something unknown and uncertain. It is also a basic truth that men part reluctantly with myths to which they have given much faith and loyalty. If there is confusion and bitterness within the international system today, there is still that irrational hope for the universal victory of the 1917 Revolution which has sparked the Soviet imagination for a half-century. Stemming from this visionary streak and the understandable reluctance to abandon a memorable revolutionary heritage, the Soviet ability to cling to a theory against all evidence and even to sustain hope against reasonable expectations, stubbornly persists. Rather than blueprints for action or even declarations of intentions, however, the greater part of Soviet ideological pontifications must be emitted to serve a deeply felt psychological need at home, a practice which cannot be terminated either easily or soon. As Brzezinski and Huntington have so aptly summarized it in their comparative study of the Soviet and American political systems:

Perhaps the most conclusive evidence of
the role that ideology will play in the Soviet
future comes from the experience of the
American past. The basic elements in the
American political creed have remained
relatively unchanged since the beginning of
the nineteenth century. Lockian ideas of
liberty, Jeffersonian concepts of democracy,
eighteenth-century ideals of the rights of
man, and laissez-faire doctrines of private property still pre-empt the American
mind. In 1789 who would have thought that
these ideas . . . would still prevail in a
crowded, organized, industrialized con-
tinental empire one hundred and fifty years
later? . . . The continuing vitality in America of the liberal-democratic ideas of 1800
suggests that it may be some while before
the Marxist-Leninist ideology of 1900 ceases
to exert its influence on the Soviet political system. [11]

Meanwhile, if the CPSU can no longer radically restruc-
ture society according to doctrinal ideals, it can at least retool
itself in accordance with the pressing demands of society. Fit-
ful and sporadic administrative overhauls and constant manipulation of the Party's structure reveal a desire to bring the
regime into a more efficacious relationship with the needs of
the Soviet populace. As a consequence, the concrete expression of Soviet ideology perforce becomes the promotion of
welfare at home, the support of Communist revolution abroad
(or, in its contemporary form, wars of national liberation),
and the development of Marxist-Leninist solidarity among the
ruling-party states of the international socialist system—in
short, a concerted effort to infuse fresh life into aging dogmas

through a trifold policy which relegates some highly significant tests of doctrinal rectitude and revolutionary elan to
"progressive" relationships with Eastern Europe.

Such tests are today a major issue because the struggle
for doctrinal unity is being waged internationally, and because the continued force of Marxist-Leninist ideology, influence, and prestige becomes an increasingly vital justification for the regime in the USSR as industrialization is
accomplished and the Soviet State shows no signs of withering away. This means that the continued relevance of
Communist Party rule, indeed of communism itself, rests
upon the utility of its fundamental ideology as a catechism
for rapid-pace development outside the USSR. Notable
fidelity to this objective was expressed in 1962 by Chairman
Khrushchev:

> Now with the emergence of socialism beyond
> the boundaries of . . . [the USSR], we ob-
> serve an unparalleled process of working
> people joining in the effort to build a new
> society on the scale of a world system . . . .
> This process only began in the course of
> the past fifteen years when new relations
> between the peoples and new forms of the
> all-round co-operation of the socialist
> countries were taking shape . . . . A
> steadily growing significance is acquired
> by the . . . things that unite . . . all the
> people taking part in building the new life,
> namely their common interests in the fight
> to ensure the victory and consolidation of
> socialism and communism on a world scale,
> and their common Marxist-Leninist ideology.

> The socialist commonwealth now has tre-
> mendous new possibilities for exerting an
> influence on world development. And this
> cannot but be a source of joy to us Commu-
> nists. But as internationalists we realize
> that this imposes also great obligations.
> On the socialist countries and on their
> Marxist-Leninist parties rests a truly his-
> torical responsibility so that these possi-
> bilities be used in full measure both in each
> country and on the scale of our entire sys-
> tem. [12]

Whatever the self-declared gains of socialism beyond the
boundaries of the USSR, the Soviets must face many enlarged
and troublesome challenges in both foreign and domestic policy,
owing largely to their Party's theoretical underpinnings. <u>First,</u>
a revolutionary regime cannot remain revolutionary if the interna
tionalist future to which it is so fervently committed remains
beyond realization. Furthermore, when international communism demonstrates grave contradictions and discrepancies, a
disruptive effect is exerted upon the heretofore unquestioned
legitimacy and future of the political system in the USSR. At
least this much was broadly and defensively hinted when on January 6, 1961, Chairman Khrushchev referred to shortcomings
in Party activity and strongly reaffirmed the Soviet dedication
to proletarian internationalism:

> The Soviet Union has always sacredly ful-
> filled and is fulfilling its international duty,
> placing the unity of countries of the social-
> ist camp, of the international Communist
> movement, above all else. Our Commu-
> nist Party will continue to adhere to this,
> its immutable policy. [13]

48

The history of Soviet foreign relations shows, of course, that the unity of the international Communist movement has not been placed above all else—i. e. , not above the more specific and pressing national interests of the USSR. Chairman Khrushchev's claim is nevertheless significant for its desire to view the Soviet Union's exercise of internationalist responsibilities in as favorable light as possible. Expressing on the same occasion a tone of reservation about "mutual relations between the fraternal parties, " he then went on to say:

> In the Communist movement there are no parties that are superior or subordinate. All Communist Parties are equal and independent . . . .
>
> There have grown up in the Communist Parties hardened Marxist-Leninist cadres capable of leading their own parties, their countries. However, in practice, as is well known, the CPSU does not give directives to any other parties. The fact that we are called the leader gives no advantages either to our party or to other parties. On the contrary, it only creates difficulties.14

Second, the tenets of Marxist-Leninist ideology, long under attack by the forces of nationalism, are increasingly vulnerable from another direction. The Weltanschauung of the contemporary generation was never tempered in the crucibles of revolution. Largely because Soviet youth sees the Revolution in the light of its own experience and not that of 1917 or earlier, there is an intensification of the ideological crisis at home, rooted in impressive domestic successes

and the ameliorative effects of time and travel, all of which
induce complacency and clash with the revolutionary imperative to forge ahead. Put quite simply, the Soviet people would
seem to prefer one pie in the hand to several in the sky. Such
a preference, if it is not to impede the race into the future,
is best manipulated and held in check by fresh increments of
dynamism and purpose. One recourse is to up the bonds of
ideological unity—a task which stimulates a strong impulse to
seek doctrinal confirmation in the international sphere. The
result could be ambitious foreign policies which, if too militant and bold, may jeopardize efforts to accumulate the domestic abundance essential for the transition to communism. In
view of avowed objectives, the Soviet Union urgently needs
peace and economic plenty at home, both of which could be
endangered by pressing international responsibilities, unless
of course such responsibilities were geographically contiguous
and productive of minimal risks. A convenient alternative,
often practiced by the Soviets, is to verbalize revolution ener-
getically but calmly forbear in the face of its unacceptable
risks.

In short, one towering foreign policy issue for the Kremlin today is not the defense of the USSR from without, but
rather from within, chiefly because of the ideological void
which develops as the futuristic goals of Marxism-Leninism
become less relevant to the functions of Communist Party
rule and increasingly dependent upon what transpires in the
affairs of loyal system members. It is only speculation, but
if the regime, say, in Poland were suddenly transformed into

a two-party parliamentary democracy, the political system in the USSR would be immediately buffeted by a current of doubt and confusion that conceivably could snatch away the remaining internationalist planks upon which so much of the Soviet Party program is built. One must hasten to add that such a development is hardly probable; but as a hypothetical case, it serves to stress the point that the political process in Moscow is uncommonly dependent upon what occurs in Warsaw, Prague, and all the other ostensible showcases for Marxism-Leninism. In this important sense, it is not the withering away of the state but the withering away of a once dynamic and cohesive ideology that causes the greatest discomfort and poses the rankling task of continually providing appealing and relevant guideposts for the future. What continues to rest so precariously is the once invulnerable internationalist platform for the militantly organized vanguard of Soviet society.

Of momentous significance, the 1956 landmark Soviet decision regarding Hungary was particularly instructive in highlighting the Soviet leadership's sensitivity to the international imperatives and responsibilities of this platform. As Chairman Khrushchev said:

> Comrades! Believe me, the decision was difficult, but we could not stand by indifferently when brazen fascist elements began to brutally attack workers, peasants, Communists and other fine representatives of the Hungarian working people . . . when the

> counter-revolution tried to drown the social-
> ist gains of the Hungarian working people in
> the blood of the people . . . .
>
> In giving aid to the Hungarian people in rout-
> ing the forces of counterrevolution, we ful-
> filled our international duty. [15]

Whatever may be said about the deviations of the Yugo-
slavs and Albanians (or even the Chinese), in the Soviet view
these nations practice forms of national communism; that is,
they are at least headed in the "right" direction. By contrast,
however, the direction in which the Hungarian revolutionaries
were leading their country appeared anti-Communist, even
pro-capitalist, and out of the system altogether. Although the
bid of the Freedom Fighters for greater national independence
was not a violation of Soviet territory, it most assuredly was
an attack upon seminal doctrine and the frequent revolutionary
prognostications of Soviet leaders. Since the alleged wave of
the future is said to be ineluctably driven forward, Hungary
could not be permitted passage into uncertain political limbo.
A monumental historical task could be performed if the "wave
of the future" could be so dammed from behind that it would
never recede. Once again, the ideological stakes were poign-
antly clear: a regime once Marxist-Leninist must not be permitted to atrophy or become anything else, for this would mar
the historical pattern of forward momentum and the necessary
potential for doctrinal confirmation. The success of Hungarian
workers in defying their "Workers' Government" was certainly embarrassing; and with the chance that the country might

have become a hotbed of great-power rivalry and disorder, Soviet decision-makers were forced into acts of military suppression which were manifestly unpopular but vital to Marxist-Leninist solidarity within their East European preserve. In addition to the obvious military ramifications, what clearly hung in the balance was a direct challenge to fundamental doctrine, with the possibility for irreparable damage to Soviet prestige and ultimate regime security.

In a somewhat belated historical sense, Lenin was almost right: theoretically speaking, a full circle is being completed. Although foreign upheavals did not materialize to support the Bolshevik Revolution, they must now arise to provide ultimate confirmation for the regime which it created. Both Lenin and Trotsky originally argued that the Revolution in Russia could eventually succeed only with the dynamic support of proletarian revolts in nations where capitalism was either ripe or weak. Stalin reversed the hierarchy of priorities and promoted a policy of socialism in one country which, while not ignoring the utility of an international Communist movement, placed almost exclusive emphasis upon strengthening the Soviet state at high speed. It was his belief that the Soviet Union should make world revolution possible instead of being dependent upon it. Such efforts, of course, were not misplaced, for it would have been well-nigh impossible to ward off German incursions during World War II and impose Soviet controls upon Eastern Europe without the reliable foundations of an industrial state.

Stalin's priority is of particular interest because, if we are to believe the interminable spate of official Kremlin pronouncements, socialism in one country is not the final goal of Soviet politics. International communism is. For this the maxims of Lenin and Trotsky may be invoked once again to show that the ultimate realization of Soviet aims must necessarily be sustained by foreign events—that is to say, the primary virtues of Marxism-Leninism are to be demonstrated in international relations. This is what Bolshevik leaders articulated during the founding of their state, and since then both Stalin and Khrushchev have enunciated the importance of areas outside the USSR—Stalin in the name of bourgeois-nationalist movements at the 19th Party Congress (1952), and Khrushchev in terms of "a vast zone of peace" at the 20th (1956). Especially relevant to such outside interests are the subtle Soviet pressures toward ideological fulfillment, and the heightened significance of Eastern Europe as an area where communism can potentially be demonstrated as a mature international phenomenon supporting the predictions and continued legitimacy of the CPSU.

Though successes in industrialization and a burgeoning standard of living are persuasive plaudits for communism, they also quite paradoxically generate within the Soviet system an interest and incentive structure which promotes national development on its own merits. What, then, would be the justification for the self-arrogated exclusiveness of the CPSU? The challenge which confronts the Soviet leadership with all its trappings of tutelage and elitism is that the verity of Soviet social policy must also be tested in areas where Marxism-Leninism is in earlier formative stages, and in the under-developed parts of the world where endemic disorder may be cited as proof that the forces which are supporting the "wave of the future" bear boundless vitality and the seeds of suc-cess. Herein lies the evidence of activity on the international level for which Lenin hoped during 1918-1922 and which he deemed vital to the future of the Soviet regime. The validity of his thesis must now be tested outside the Soviet Union, and as a matter of dedicated policy, not only in distant regions but also in an adjacent area where the Soviets have long been promoting efforts to moderate historically troublesome re-lationships.

At no time was this dedication voiced with more clarity and dramatic flourish than in 1958 when Chairman Khrushchev in his inimitable style addressed the Hungarians:

> Comrades, we are working hand in hand with
> you to build communism. The Soviet people
> will come to communism together with you,
> the working people of Hungary. It is out of
> the question that we, Communists and inter-
> nationalists of the Soviet Union, the first to
> seize power and to engage in the great cause
> of communist construction, should come to
> communism alone, and, to use a figure of
> speech, should eat ham every day while the
> rest look on and lick their chops. That would
> be wrong.
>
> Where would the proletarian solidarity, the
> internationalism, of that socialist country
> be then? The country with the more developed

economy, capable of raising the living standard of its people still higher, must by all
means help the other socialist countries to
level out with time. All the countries will
rise to the level of the foremost ones, which
are also not going to mark time. We must
enter the Communist world all together. [16]

Realistically speaking, and with allowances for Khrushchevian rhetoric, how may such a grand enterprise be effected at the present turbulent juncture in Marxist-Leninist
international relations?

THE ROLE OF EAST EUROPEAN
INTERNATIONAL ORGANIZATIONS

Recent years have witnessed a significant regularization
of organizational relations among the Marxist-Leninist states
of Eastern Europe, which for a number of postwar years were
subjected to informal and indirect Stalinist controls that pro-
voked nationalist sensitivities and made a sham of frequent
declarations of proletarian unity and fraternal cooperation. 1

Historically, the Soviets have never displayed great hopes
for any but their own international political organizations. Although in theory this position has not precluded flexibility when
deemed advantageous, in practice there have been many past
difficulties, not the least of which included efforts to convince
the Western Powers that the Soviet Union could be a worthy
ally in international conciliation and other projects of commonly expressed interest. For example, the efforts of Foreign Ministers Chicherin and Litvinov to conduct a peaceful
foreign policy in the capitals of the Western World during the
20's and 30's clashed quite conspicuously with the bellicose
pronouncements and revolutionary aspirations of the Comintern, to which the Soviet Union was also dedicated. In the
main, the underlying Soviet attitude toward international organizations has rested upon the conviction that mankind will

be guided to world government and eventually to statelessness through regional arrangements of Communist fabrication. Practical necessities in mid-century, however, have arrested any early realization of this hope, and there exists today a variety of organizational relationships among Communist states which belies the monolithism and centralism long attributed to the Soviet political process.

Contemporary organizational relationships in the international socialist system contrast sharply with earlier experiences. The Comintern was a tightly knit body: it held world congresses, had an executive committee in permanent session, established a permanent bureaucracy, possessed its own centers of administration separate from national parties, and operated an elaborate propaganda network. From its inception, it fell under the shadow of the CPSU and, after the mid-twenties, functioned primarily as an arm of Soviet foreign policy. When the purges of the 30's decimated its ranks, and the Polish Communist Party in particular was dissolved and its leadership removed, the scope and accomplishment of Soviet controls became frightfully apparent. Perhaps for this reason, the Cominform of 1947-1956 was never more than a pale shadow of its earlier model. The Chinese never joined, and notwithstanding broad integrative and informational purposes, it did little more than publish a propaganda journal and malign Tito. When the "fraternal parties" met after the harrowing events of 1956 (as in Moscow, November 1957) and contemplated formal institutions for strengthening unity, past encounters could not have but cautioned against hasty decisions. Several of the participants expressed polite misgivings, and the matter was curtly dropped. In view of festering Soviet disagreement with the Chinese and Albanians, and almost certain Polish and Rumanian opposition, it is unlikely that a permanent directing organ on the model of the Comintern (or even the Cominform) will ever be created again.

Yielding to necessity for more than a decade now, the Soviets have acted in a number of ways to remove the greatest irritants of their presence in Eastern Europe and to grant varying degrees of independence, naturally favored by the trends in world politics since World War II. Almost simultaneously, organizational measures promoting stability and integration have become genuinely important. With the days of sterile rigidity and the Soviet Empire gone, the goal of East European elites has been to keep the basic system together and their privileged positions intact. To this end, they have voiced expressions of solidarity and common purpose through various organizational devices—a useful enterprise when it is understood that in the current Marxist-Leninist purview, socialist nations in various stages of development will continue to exist as separate political entities during the period of Communist construction, presumably until the international socialist system becomes universal. The question is how best to express and facilitate this interim phase.

The most recent program of the CPSU, particularly Section VI, is instrumental in disclosing Soviet thinking along these lines:

> The fact that socialist revolutions took place
> at different times and that the economic and
> cultural levels of the countries concerned
> are dissimilar, predetermines the nonsimul-
> taneous completion of socialist construction
> in those countries and their nonsimultane-
> ous entry into the period of the full-scale
> construction of communism. Nevertheless,
> the fact that the socialist countries are de-
> veloping as members of a single world
> socialist system enables them to reduce the
> time necessary for the construction of so-
> cialism and offers them the prospect of
> effecting the transition to communism—
> more or less simultaneously, within one and
> the same historical epoch.[2]

Communists have shown little initiative or originality in organizing their own international agencies. Existing institutionalized cooperation has been largely in imitation of, and response to, similar measures in the West. There are three system-wide organizations—the Organization for the Collaboration of Railways, the International Broadcasting Organization, and the Joint Institute of Nuclear Research at Dubna, USSR—and two which are less than system-wide and centered in Eastern Europe—the Warsaw Treaty Organization and the Council for Mutual Economic Cooperation (COMECON). [3]

Interestingly enough, whether by design or because of Chinese refusals, Asian ruling-party states have not been formally linked together in cooperative integrative enterprises; and with the exception of the Mongolian People's Republic, they have not been part of the multilateral political, military, or economic agencies (Cominform, WTO, COMECON centered in Eastern Europe. Aside from other significant differences, the organizational distinction between Asian and East European communism has quite naturally reinforced the formation and consolidation of an Asian subsystem (minus Mongolia) with its apparent focus in China, and an East European subsystem (minus Albania) focused upon the USSR.

There is no hard evidence that any of these organizations were created as nuclei of possibly worldwide agencies. Rather, as functionally specific groups, they arose as collectivist instruments for answering concrete regional problems. The WTO and COMECON are particularly engrossing because of their proximity to the USSR, their special relevance to Soviet domestic policy, their utility in regularizing Soviet predominance in East European affairs, and their role in preserving at least a semblance of international Communist cohesion in a period of cumulative diversity and intense ideological disputes. A brief analysis of each organization follows.

WTO

The Warsaw Treaty Organization was established on May 14, 1955, largely as an answer to German membership in NATO and the West European Union. In its early days, the WTO functioned chiefly to institutionalize the close ties between the USSR and its satellites, formalized in the Treaty's provision preventing members from participating in any other alliance system which would be "incompatible with the purposes of the present treaty."[4] More recently the organization's main emphasis has fallen upon habitual excoriation of

West Germany for its allegedly revanchist military projects within NATO, which in turn has been accused of restoring West Germany to the command of Hitlerite generals and equipping it with rockets and nuclear weapons. [5]

The WTO Political Consultation Committee, empowered to create other multilateral organs, has established a commission for foreign policy coordination and a secretariat consisting of representatives from each member state. Formal meetings serve primarily as forums during which common approaches to defense problems are enunciated, with the USSR delegated as the pact's chief spokesman. Although the Committee has the authority to discuss and decide general questions regarding the strengthening of defense power and the organization of armed forces, on the basis of available evidence, it has not been an active policy-making body, certainly not in the sense that both formal and informal gatherings of high Party officials have proved to be.

Frankly, given the evidence at hand, it is difficult to see that WTO has a defense policy of its own. As the Soviet contingent of the joint military force outweighs the contributions of all other members together, the strictly military significance of the organization falls more properly within the general scope of the Soviet Union's own defense policy. Nevertheless, the organization has its own commander in chief, a staff for the joint armed forces composed of personnel permanently appointed from member states, and permanent delegations of general staffs from each signatory power. Each delegation within the joint command retains its national identity. There is as yet no firm indication that a fully unified international command and the "higher forms" of close cooperation have materialized. By and large, national armies have been fully subordinated to the dominant power and presence of the Soviet Union, and as expected, military planning and maneuvers have assured prominent command positions to Soviet officers. At no time during WTO's history was Soviet primacy given more poignant testimony than in the fall of 1956, when in its singularly most far-reaching postwar operation to date, the Soviet Army was galvanized into discharging its international duty under the provisions of the pact. [6]

Aside from the Soviet Union's unilaterally assumed responsibility for protecting the internal socialist order in each of the member states, there is also the larger commitment to defend the outer frontiers of the pact's signatories from international encroachments. Reaffirming this commitment, [7] Pravda on May 14, 1960 stated:

> Today the whole world has had an opportunity to be assured that anyone who dares to encroach upon the inviolability of the Soviet Union's borders, as well as those of other socialist countries, will receive a crushing rebuff. The Warsaw Treaty Organization is based on the principle of all for one and one for all. The Soviet government has frequently stated that the borders of all its true friends— the socialist countries—will be defended by the Soviet Union exactly as if they were its own borders. This is how we understand proletarian internationalism, and this is how all the peoples of the socialist countries understand it.

63

Although the Warsaw Treaty Organization provided somewhat vaguely for Soviet bases abroad, no agreement in Stalin's time officially sanctioned the stationing of Soviet troops on foreign soil. Since the revolutions of 1956, however, Soviet garrisons have been situated in Eastern Europe under strictly bilateral agreements which use the Warsaw Treaty as a point of reference but obviously raise some embarrassing questions as to its genuine multilateral effectiveness. For example, the overarching treaty has not proved sufficiently comprehensive to encompass all military arrangements (occupational included) among its eight members.

There are a number of important military agreements outside the confines of WTO. The Soviet-East German Treaty of September 20, 1955, defined relations between the two states and granted the Ulbricht regime full freedom to make decisions on all questions pertaining to East Germany's domestic and foreign policy, including relations with the Federal Republic of Germany. On March 12, 1957, a formal agreement was concluded providing for the presence of Soviet troops in East Germany.[8] The Polish-Soviet Treaty of December 17, 1956 formalized for the first time a situation which had existed in fact since World War II. The provisions governing the number, status, and location of Soviet troops on Polish territory were explicit and designed to mollify deep-seated Polish grievances. The agreement imposed stringent restrictions upon unilateral operations, prohibited the use of troops for political purposes, required greater accommodation to the wishes of the Polish government, and made Soviet personnel

64

and dependents subject to Polish law.[9] These concessions
were followed by similar accords with Rumania and Hungary
(April 15 and May 27, respectively), both versions of which
notably lacked the Polish provision for control over entry and
exit of Soviet troops.[10]

Considering WTO's original prospectus, the chief contemporary significance has narrowed substantially and would
seem to be as follows: it is a formalized effort to unite the
states of Eastern Europe in a common purpose, primarily
against the threat of potential German aggression; it serves
to limit the exercise of some aspects of their sovereignty,
particularly in matters of self-defense; and it provides extra
opportunities to articulate ostentatious unanimity and support
of Soviet policies on issues of common interests—on the one
hand, vehement condemnation of American war efforts in
Vietnam and continued "revanchist plots" in West Germany,
and on the other, repeated proposals for an all-European conference to discuss security and East-West cooperation, dis-
mantling of foreign military bases and withdrawal of troops,
a scaling down of all armed forces, the creation of denucle-
arized zones (including the nonaccess to nuclear weapons by
West Germany), and the recognition of two German states.[11]

A balance sheet of the pact's conferences and activities
would have to show that very little in support of original expressed objectives has been accomplished. Particularly as a
result of the general Cold War detente which appears to have
coursed through Europe, the underlying reasons for the founding of WTO have diminished in urgency. Although periodic

top-level consultations have as yet yielded little more than pious affirmations of socialist internationalism, at the risk of oversimplification it can be said that it is in these that the principal utility and relevance of the organization are to be found. For example, reduced to the simplest authoritative terms:

> It is impossible to overestimate the international role of the mighty Soviet Armed Forces in insuring the defense potential of the Socialist countries. . . . All the practical activities of the Warsaw Treaty Organization, the Political Consultative Committee and its other agencies furnish a graphic example of Socialist internationalism in action. [12]

COMECON

At the present time, the Council for Mutual Economic Cooperation is the most important single international organization for actively shaping socialist unity and formalizing the Soviet Union's presence and influence in Eastern Europe. In the troublesome post-1956 period of political stabilization, it served as a much-needed forum for multilateral consultations, and since then it has provided the principal focus for cooperative activities designed to build a "world socialist market" while simultaneously sustaining political and ideological cohesion among East European system members. Today, it constitutes the most feasible framework within which some form of genuinely international Communist society may emerge. Devoting exceptional emphasis to the Council's role in economic development among system members, Chairman Khrushchev in his address of January 6, 1961, offered a significant political note which has contemporary significance only if it is understood that the ambit of its practical application has in reality been reduced to the Soviet-East European subsystem.

>In the part of the earth occupied by the world Socialist system, the prototype of a new society for all mankind is being created. This places a particular responsibility on the Communist Parties of all the Socialist countries.
>
>The countries of the world Socialist system are coming closer and closer together, strengthening their cooperation in all spheres of activity . . . . The more highly developed and economically powerful countries give unselfish, brotherly help to the economically underdeveloped . . . . At the same time, we consider it our duty to point out that the fraternal countries of socialism, in their turn, cooperate with the Soviet Union in the development of our economy.
>
>Coordination of national economic plans has become the basic form of combining the productive efforts of Socialist countries at the present stage. It is in the interest of all countries to perfect this work, particularly in connection with the task of working out the long-term plan for the expansion of the national economies of Socialist countries. The consolidation of the common economic base of the world Socialist system, the creation of a material base for a more or less simultaneous transition of the peoples of the Socialist system to communism will be achieved more rapidly to the degree that the internal resources of each country are fully mobilized within this system, to the degree that the

advantages of the Socialist international
division of labor are used more ade-
quately. . . .[13]

Efforts at economic coordination and integration in Eastern Europe can be traced to the establishment of the Soviet
system of satellites at the end of World War II. Although between 1945 and 1948 some autonomous development of individual national economies was permitted, the whole of the
early postwar period was mainly characterized by repeated
Soviet intervention and exploitation on a broad scale. The
chief methods consisted in transfers of goods and services
which accrued to the USSR as a result of the defeat of Germany,
outright seizures of plants and equipment under the guise of
war booty, the imposition of exploitative trade schemes through
the formation of so-called joint-stock companies with East
European states, and finally, Soviet purchases of raw materials and produce at prices lower than those prevailing on
world markets. The manipulation of joint-stock companies
and their subsequent liquidation provided the primary means
by which the Soviets realized significant profits, particularly
when shares in these enterprises were finally sold to the satellite states on terms highly unfavorable to the purchasers.

It soon became clear that a Kremlin-directed trade mechanism was not of itself forging economies into a purposeful
integrated whole based on a rational division of labor; and the
lack of such integration was only causing enormous waste and
hampering the growth of all the satellite states. Realizing the
urgency of the problem, Communist leaders finally initiated

efforts toward multilateral cooperation by employing methods more compatible with long-range economic and political objectives. In January 1949 the establishment of an intergovernmental Council for Mutual Economic Cooperation was announced. The founding participants were Bulgaria, Czechoslovakia, Hungary, Poland, Rumania, and the USSR. Albania joined in February, and in September 1950 East Germany became a member. Since 1956, China, North Korea, and North Vietnam have been accorded "observer status." Mongolia was admitted at the Council's 15th session in June 1962. Cuba apparently began to participate as an "observer" in 1963, and Yugoslavia received "non-member participant status with equal rights" in September 1964.[14]

At the first plenary session in April 1949, the Council was described as an open organization which other European countries could join if they desired to participate in broad economic collaboration. This principle was tested when Yugoslavia first applied for admission and was promptly rejected with a blunt answer from Moscow:

> The Council for Mutual Economic Aid was not founded for normal economic cooperation, such as exists, for example, between the USSR and Belgium or Holland. The Council was founded for economic cooperation on the broad foundation of those nations which conduct an honest and friendly policy with each other.[15]

The Council prospectus emphasized the advantages of broad economic collaboration and mutual aid on a basis of equality.

Members were to coordinate economic plans, establish joint investment programs, and divide productive forces according to the material and historical requirements of each country. [16]

Not surprisingly, the results of organizational efforts were at first almost nil. Beginning in 1949, all of the states initiated long-term economic plans which in essential aspects duplicated one another; and the deeply ingrained autarkic policies of the past continued without visible changes. Iron, steel, and heavy industry were emphasized regardless of national resources, and beyond the expansion of limited bilateral trade agreements, Stalin allowed the Council little meaningful authority.

After Stalin's passing, a turn in economic developments became a more genuine possibility. In line with general efforts toward establishing greater unity and productivity, there emerged a somewhat more dedicated and rational policy aimed toward the development of the East European bloc's economic potential across the board. Although such a policy would normally entail the organization of production on a basis of comparative advantages, progress along these lines was a near impossibility. In the first place, autarkic planning, which the USSR had inspired in the postwar years, created a fixed dependence on Soviet raw materials and markets, thus impeding meaningful integrative exchanges. Furthermore, the fact that all the satellite states attempted to follow the same pattern in economic development resulted in gross duplication and eliminated the possibility of dovetailing economies. Economic autarky was further enhanced by the unreliability of supply sources and markets within the satellite complex as a whole; and the fact that domestic prices were completely divorced from external markets ruled out the possibility of an effectively operative system of comparative costs. In such a closed system, how was one to discover the cheapest source of supply and channel resources accordingly?

Gradually, it became obvious that a genuine coordination of economies could not be stimulated by fragmentary adjustments of certain production targets. Nor were the declarations of high-level conferences enough to accomplish the sharing and integration projected so enthusiastically but without the concessions necessary for even minimal success. The result was that the blueprint for a truly unified East European economy did not begin to emerge until 1958.

Three years later, in his speech to the 22nd Party Congress, Chairman Khrushchev expounded dramatically on the economic achievements of the international socialist system and declared that a decisive stage in the economic competition between socialism and capitalism had arrived:

> The growing fraternal rapprochement between the socialist countries, together with their political and economic consolidation, constitutes one of the decisive factors of the strength and durability of the world socialist system. We joined forces voluntarily in order to march forward together. The union was not imposed on us by anyone. We need it as much as we need air.
>
> The chief thing now is, by consistently developing the economy of each socialist

country and all of them collectively, to
achieve preponderance of the socialist
world's absolute volume of production
over that of the capitalist world. This
will be a great historic victory for socialism. [17]

Speaking in the fall of 1962, regarding the international
division of labor, Chairman Khrushchev stated:

Socialist international division of labor
and wide specialization and co-ordination
of production provide the national economies of the socialist countries with the
broadest opportunities for the most fruit-
ful development; the various economies,
supplementing one another, will gradually
merge into a single streamlined economic
complex with each having its own place and
functions and in which each country, each
people, will have an even stronger foundation for solving the national tasks of socialist construction. [18]

Since 1962, the Council has consisted of a Council of
Governmental Delegations, which holds sessions at infre-
quent intervals, determines the most important matters of
policy, and creates new agencies; the Conference of Representatives, permanently residing in Moscow and responsible
for administrative and technical operations, including the
supervision of the secretariat and standing commissions; and
an Executive Committee specifically created to promote integration and supranational planning by deputy premiers in
charge of economic development in each member state.
Finally, a varying number of special standing commissions,
representing major branches of the economy, have been

established to carry out proposals which must be agreed upon unanimously.

Developments of the most recent years indicate diligent Council efforts in a wide number of carefully delimited projects. At the same time, significantly more liberal trends have been operative, both in terms of flexible credit and longer-term trade arrangements in which genuinely coordinated planning and mutual agreements have been distinct features. Such agreements, often negotiated between groups of Council members, continue to be accompanied by significant exchanges of scientific knowledge between national institutes and academies, and considerable scientific and technical collaboration on a wide variety of commonly faced economic problems. The more celebrated Council projects include the "Friendship Oil Pipeline," linking the rich petroleum-producing areas of the Soviet Union with East Germany, Poland, Czechoslovakia, and Hungary; an international grid designed to integrate the power systems of all COMECON members through a Central Control Board which commenced operations in Prague on January 1, 1963; and multilateral cooperation in the production and distribution of rolled ferrous metals through Intermetall, an organization founded with the objective of linking the metallurgical operations of Poland, Czechoslovakia, and Hungary. [19]

Regarding steps toward more efficient financial arrangements, Pravda reported on October 24, 1963, that Council members had signed an agreement for multilateral clearings in transferable rubles and agreed on the establishment

of the International Bank for Economic Cooperation.   Under
the terms,

> . . . accounts connected with the mutual
> delivery and other payments between con-
> tracting parties will be settled in conver-
> sion rubles as of January 1, 1964 . . . .
> Each contracting party will, when conclud-
> ing trade agreements, insure a balance of
> payment in conversion rubles with all other
> contracting parties within the calendar
> year. [20]

More recently, it was reported that, as of July 1, 1966, a
percentage of the Bank's holdings in Moscow will be converted
into gold, thus contributing to the establishment of at least a
partially convertible ruble. [21]

Finally, all this has been provided architectural promi-
nence through the erection of a spectacular thirty-story building (on the banks of the Moscow River) to house the Council's
administrative activities.   According to Pravda, August 24,
1964, this international construction project, symbolizing
fraternal cooperation within the socialist commonwealth, is
to be part of a magnificent complex of only the most modern
equipment and facilities, topped by the national flags of Council members.

Operating within the confines of COMECON, the Danube
Commission has increasingly become an international technical agency, with very few if any activities devoted to political purposes.   Since the organization includes a non-Marxist-
Leninist participant—Austria (West Germany has received
"observer status" only)—it really cannot be viewed as an

institution designed to promote unity among strictly system
members in Eastern Europe. Nevertheless, at least one
extraordinary project is deserving of note. Yugoslavia and
Rumania have made concerted efforts toward erecting a $400
million dam and lock system which will speed and multiply
traffic through the famous Iron Gates sector of their Danube
River frontier. Plans include the building of a hydroelectric
plant which will be one of the five largest in the world and
will provide both countries with all the power they need,
plus a surplus for export. The project is especially impressive because it was undertaken against considerable opposition by other Commission members and consequently had
to be a major investment decision by two Balkan states outside the framework of COMECON. Even though there is
considerable dependence upon Soviet loans, there is no denying that both nations have underscored their ability and
willingness to take action serving their individual national,
as well as common, interests. Resultant transactions have
tended to mitigate the imposing proximity of the Soviet Union
and calm the hotbed of historically vexatious Balkan politics.

All of these cooperative activities merit close attention
for their utility in promoting the growth of East European
economies separately and as a whole, and beyond this, their
potential values to whatever survives of common political objectives. If one takes the plethora of Soviet pronouncements
and predictions seriously, however, there are many problems and unresolved issues. Nikita Khrushchev's inflated

claims for a grand "more or less simultaneous entry into the higher phase of Communist society" through planned proportional development and a sort of "evening-out process" face formidable difficulties, both economic and political. [22]

Writing in the period 1959-60, Alfred Zauberman, a British economist specializing in centrally planned economies, presented a comprehensive review of problems besetting economic integration—problems which continue to be strikingly applicable today. [23] How, he asked, can planners determine which country has the best conditions for developing a certain line of production? If prices fail to reflect profit opportunities on a national level, they can hardly be used as indicators of opportunity costs and sensible investment choices for Eastern Europe as a whole. In pricing and in determining the most effective producer of certain goods, costs can be rationally arrived at if the prices on which they are based are internationally comparable. This is difficult in an area for the most part insulated economically from the rest of the world.

Although, more recently, prices for commodity exchanges were to be based on the average of world market prices for 1960-64, actual economic arrangements for the period were being projected by pairs of states mostly on a barter basis, indicating that attempts toward free-flowing multilateral trade were notably unsuccessful. Moreover, recommendations made by the Council were not enforceable by any authority, thus causing uncertainty in transactions.

In an effort to manage some of these problems, a per-

manent economic commission was established to compare
production efficiency in member countries and investigate
the vexing problems of industrial specialization, the amount
of capital required per unit of output, output per man-hour,
and overall cost per output unit. [24] A trend toward advanced
linear programming methods also ensued; but quite apart
from technical difficulties, resultant pricing policies continue
to face serious doctrinal hurdles, and there remains a whole
series of even more complicated obstacles to fusing economies based on centralized planning and a habitual orientation
toward production targets rather than markets and profits.
There is no conclusive evidence that these obstacles have
been overcome or that the lingering problem of determining
comparative economic efficiency on the basis of rational cost-
price data has been solved. According to one economic ex-
pert,

> . . . It is hard to see how a number of mono-
> lithic nationally-planned economies could be
> integrated unless they were subsumed in a
> monolithic supranationally-planned economy.
> But the nationalism of the East European
> states and their autarkic economic struc-
> ture have been too strong to allow this to
> happen. Only a militantly imperialist Rus-
> sia, intent on unifying the communist bloc,
> would have been powerful enough to force
> it through; but as we have seen it was Khrush-
> chev's Russia, not Stalin's, that perceived
> the technocratic necessity of integration . . . . [25]

Finally, all of these difficulties have been multiplied by
the tendency of each member state to propose solutions based

upon particularistic national-economic interests rather than the interests of the organization as a whole. Meetings and meetings are held and the results are always strikingly similar: "COMECON business as usual," followed by bland declarations such as, "the session of the Commission proceeded in an atmosphere of friendly mutual understanding and cooperation."

Questions logically arise: Are Soviet efforts toward economic integration leading to some form of federation? Chairman Khrushchev's widely quoted Leipzig speech of March 7, 1959, was particularly instructive in disclosing at least some long-range aspirations which have not been officially repudiated or revised by his successors. The Chairman listed all the altered and disputed frontiers of Eastern Europe—the Polish-German frontier on the Oder-Neisse, the USSR's frontiers with Poland and Rumania, the Rumanian-Hungarian frontier—and went on to dismiss any idea of trouble from them. Frontier disputes between socialist states were unimaginable, he indicated. A time would come when frontiers within the socialist camp would cease to have any meaning at all—a situation which had long existed among the republics of the Soviet Union.

> The old conceptions of borders, formed on
> the basis of bourgeois legal norms, are
> still alive, along with other survivals of
> capitalism . . . . Communist society,
> which will have an abundance of material
> and spiritual wealth, is capable of satis-
> fying the needs of every individual as well
> as of every nation . . . . In these conditions,

the old concepts of borders as such will
gradually disappear. With the victory of
communism on a worldwide scale, state
borders will disappear as Marxism-
Leninism teaches.

Extensive cooperation in all spheres of
economic, social, political, and cultural
life is developing among the sovereign
countries of the socialist camp. Speaking of the future, it seems to me that the
further development of the socialist countries will in all probability proceed along
the lines of consolidation of a single world
socialist economic system. The economic
barriers which divided our countries under
capitalism will fall one after another. The
common economic basis of world socialism
will grow stronger, eventually making the
question of borders a pointless one. [26]

This same theme was echoed by Todor Zhivkov in January
1963:

Ever-growing cooperation and unity of the
countries comprising the socialist camp
which, in perspective, will merge into a
single communist entity with a common
economy, culture, science, and with common social relationships — such is the trend
of the times.

The soundness of this thesis is fully confirmed by the fact that successful advance
by our countries is inconceivable without
their growing unity in all spheres.[27]

However consoling to the Soviet inclination toward visionary speculation, schemes for "growing unity in all spheres"
bear manifold problems. Much has been said and written

about the discriminatory policies which the USSR effected in Eastern Europe, and, no doubt, these favored the Soviet Union and may in certain cases continue to do so. For example, it should not be overlooked that if the Khrushchev era is best remembered for its acts of political liberalization and the relaxation of tensions, it is equally true that the peripatetic Soviet Chairman attempted to interfere in the economic affairs of his socialist neighbors at least as much if not more than Stalin ever did. His widely publicized proposals (August-September 1952) for a central COMECON planning organ were a logical extension of fervent hopes that strongly centralized direction would help to solve both economic and political problems of unity. Despite the Chairman's personal attachment to nothing short of producing economic miracles, however, COMECON did not fulfill the grandiose programs of its chief promoter. Instead, the proposals for a clearer division of labor based on national specialization induced hesitancy and rift among Council members. At a summit conference in July 1963, he finally agreed to shelve his supernational schemes.

For their part, leaders of the East European states recognize that economic integration in which sovereign frontiers disappear will induce Soviet hegemony over their nations; and although there are sober declarations that COMECON is not a supranational organization and that it does not affect national sovereignties, there is much reason to believe that it will operate to do just that. There is tacit recognition that integration will be consummated only if and when the East European economies are directed as a single unit, according to a comprehensive plan to be drawn up and implemented from one center of authority. And it is precisely this possibility that bodes ill for individual nation-states, in which there are vivid memories of the Soviet Union's past intrusions in practically every sphere of political, economic, and social life. For this reason, even perfectly logical economic measures such as international specialization or multilateral trade are greeted with great sensitivity and suspicion.

These reservations in their aggregate really add up to the delicate matter of balance among participants in any cooperative effort. Fundamental to the Council's abundant shortcomings, and the certain prospect of more to come, is the overwhelming preponderance of the Soviet Union. If the USSR has constituted the primary motor force in COMECON, it has also served as an insurmountable obstacle to genuine and effective international integration. Enormously wealthy, powerful and secure, 230 million strong, and unquestionably predominant in East European affairs, the Soviet Union is eight times larger in population than any other Council member (to say nothing of GNP and other factors making for national power), and would therefore clearly dominate any supranational planning body, thus relegating other members to perpetual subordination. Indeed, there is every reason to fear that, if permitted, the regime in Moscow could itself function as a supranational authority. All this smacks too much of the past to be accepted with equanimity.

Ultimately, of course, the success or failure of integration in Eastern Europe is a political question. The idea arose out of the shattering upheavals that followed Stalin's passing. Correctly perceiving the technological and political values of cooperative planning, Soviet leaders responded by abandoning militant Stalinist imperialism, intent on welding the bloc together by force, for a more wholehearted emphasis upon bilateral and multilateral arrangements designed to strengthen political bonds which were increasingly subjected to stress. There is no gainsaying the dominant position of the rich and intrusive Soviet state; but the perpetuation of its privileged position through an extensive net of formal organizational arrangements, tailored to ease relationships originally imposed under stress, requires a shift in perspectives all around.

Today, projects within the framework of COMECON have a stronger chance because Chairman Khrushchev succeeded in consolidating and maintaining Soviet power over Eastern Europe without the most blatant irritants of garrison tactics and constant interventionism. Economic integration under the auspices of the most important international organization of Eastern Europe has at least the potential of rendering that consolidation more or less permanent. This does not mean a subtle restoration of Soviet empire in Eurasia, even if that were possible. Rather, it suggests that formal institutional relationships can be utilized to relieve the evolution from an imperialist personal dictatorship to something considerably more reciprocal and complex. Indeed whatever

82

its shortcomings, regionalism is a rational, if less dramatic, way of maintaining Soviet predominance by acting to stabilize and legitimize the pervasive influence of the USSR in East European affairs. It is only reasonable to expect that organizational activity will increase in value and utility (although not necessarily in success) as the Soviet Union bends greater effort to reinforce the diminished framework within which unity must perforce be expressed. It is as if a basic theoretical foundation long held to be infallible is gradually deemed in need of props, not only because it may be inherently faulty (the Soviets certainly cannot admit this), but because times change and a variety of supports pragmatically added and subtracted as the situation demands has always been fundamental to Soviet political practice.

No adequate effort can be made here to render conclusions on how far integration has progressed or how successful in quantitative terms it has been. Evidence based upon surveys and statistical analysis of interaction among ruling-party states is as yet inconclusive. The most that may be safely said is that in the categories of political, military, and diplomatic interaction, the boundary between the East European and Asian subsystems is clear-cut. Significantly, the East European sector encompasses by far the most intense and diversified transactional activity. It is here that the idea of integration is alive and concrete efforts expended in its name. If this much can be sustained, the Soviet Union will have been at least partially successful in counteracting a good number of urgent political and ideological problems pressuring the international system as a whole.

Perhaps the most significant by-product of Soviet labors in Eastern Europe is that, however meager the tangible results relative to expansive predictions, organizational projects and functional international cooperation contribute to doctrinal validity and in turn to Soviet regime security. Apart from enhancing the Soviet Union's international image, there has been a semblance of order and mutuality in a region of historic divisiveness and rivalry. A significant difference between the approaches of East and West is that, while several West European hopefuls envisioned the Common Market as a foundation for political integration and eventual union, the process was clearly reversed in the Soviet experience where a consolidation of political power was deemed the sine qua non of future economic cooperation and integration. Organizations such as WTO and COMECON may now perform their most useful roles by helping to buttress and perpetuate the political force which gave rise to them in the first place.

Admittedly, there are limits to this. Partiinaya Zhizn', the organ of the Party's Central Committee, indicated in April 1965 that, at least for the present, the post-Khrushchev leadership has decided against the policy of adopting binding organizational forms to coordinate foreign policy among the members of COMECON and the Warsaw Pact. This was in apparent reference to the former Chairman's views that . . .

> it would be expedient to think jointly about
> those organizational forms that would make
> it possible to improve the constant exchange
> of opinions and the coordination of foreign
> policy between the members of the Council

for Mutual Economic Cooperation and the
Warsaw Pact. The commonwealth of independent socialist nations possessing
equal rights must grow stronger and develop. In this lies the guarantee of new
successes of world socialism. [28]

Moreover, Mr. Suslov's reminders regarding the need to
tighten up general proletarian discipline, stressed in a major
speech just a month before, appear to have been bypassed as
well. [29] Referring to the Comintern and Cominform, an article in Partiinaya Zhizn' stated:

Even in countries with the same social
structure, the differences are such that
only the parties operating in these countries can take them into account. Therefore in present-day conditions there exists
neither one nor several centers for the
leadership of the international Communist
movement. Attempts to revive the forms
of relations between parties which were
justified in bygone stages may produce
negative consequences and fetter the initiative of parties which are themselves
capable of solving the problems facing
their countries. [30]

More recently, General Secretary Brezhnev addressed a
Soviet-Czechoslovak friendship rally and hinted at the delicate
problems of decision-making and Soviet authority within the
Warsaw Pact, particularly in view of the pressing problems
of unity within the system. He expressed the opinion that the
structure of socialism is a dependable foundation for the
formation of "international relations of a new type." Passing over a broad range of foreign and domestic problems, he

explained that their solution would be facilitated by careful study and consideration of the pertinent experiences of other fraternal countries. Alluding to requirements for greater organizational strength, and quite possibly political and military coordination above and beyond normal defense needs, he continued:

> Present conditions place on the agenda the task to further improve (sovershenstvovat') the Warsaw Treaty Organization, that mighty instrument for the defense of the socialist world. We are all ready to work well to find the best solution for this. [31]

Politburo member Dmitri Polyansky, in his November 7, 1965 anniversary address, again referred to this need. After emphasizing COMECON's importance in strengthening the system, he declared that, "the measures for insuring the further development of the political and military cooperation of the fraternal countries within the framework of the Warsaw Treaty Organization are of great significance."[32] Coupled with the General Secretary's references, this could well be an indicator of important future reorganization for promoting greater subsystem cohesion. In apparent emulation of NATO, joint military maneuvers have been taking place since the autumn of 1961, especially among Soviet, Czechoslovakian, Polish, and East German forces. Substantial military exercises in September 1963 were for the first time conducted under the command of a non-Soviet general, and in May 1965, an "unusual conclave" of Warsaw Pact military commanders took place for a demonstration of new weapons, equipment, and tactics, and for consultation. [33]

Where do these latest authoritative statements and developments addressed to organizational unity leave the matter?
It may be true that the Soviets have been forced to abandon
close-knit arrangements on the model of the Comintern, but
what of the potential refinement of existing ventures? It is
not surprising that the accent seems to be falling upon a recognized need for new forms of economic and military cooperation, plus major activation and revisions allowing considerable
leeway for COMECON and Warsaw Pact members. Of course,
the standing offer to dissolve the Warsaw Pact if Western
Europe does the same to NATO is always prominent news; it
appears to imply that WTO is conveniently dispensable. [34]
Barring revolutionary shifts in Soviet-American relations, however, the offer would seem to be safe, since the United States
has never agreed to the built-in withdrawal principle—Soviet
troops to the USSR and US troops back across the Atlantic.
One should always welcome moves toward troop reductions
and re-engagement in both halves of Europe, but there is as
yet no convincing evidence in support of positive policy changes.

This should not negate the significance of regular reports
on the extraordinary utility of cooperative ventures whose
virtues are extolled in endless journalistic disquisitions
punctuated by hints of "new forms" of relations and glowing
references to collective successes, both actual and potential. [35] Such verbalizations are indicative of persistent and
deeply rooted trends, and no less important because of their
monotony and repetitiousness. Confirming the general thesis
of this study, their geographical orientation is remarkably

tendentious, despite Soviet interpretations to the contrary.
A revealing <u>Pravda</u> editorial of October 27, 1965 devoted
serious attention to the shifting center of the world revolutionary movement. Accepting the Chinese challenge that
this center had moved from Moscow to Peking, the Soviets
offered a fresh perspective: the center of the world revolutionary movement is a social concept (not geographical or
national), encompassing all those who are building socialism
and communism, i.e., all members of the international
socialist system. [36]

Even if one accepts the social rather than geographical
concept, the fact that the most advanced organizational efforts are centered in Eastern Europe cannot be ignored.
Pointing to the common pitfalls of supranational planning, the
Chinese may caution on behalf of national independence and
sovereignty. But it would be difficult to overlook the considerable vitality which such integrative efforts contribute
to doctrinal unity and goal vitality in the East European part
of the system, where Soviet political hegemony preceded the
victory of Chinese communism in Asia. Not that a few cooperative ventures and international organizations are decisive on any balance sheet; but the functional-institutional
approach of West European integration seems to be strikingly
applicable to the other half of Europe and in the long run is
likely to prove infinitely more productive than the methods
which prevailed a short decade ago.

INTERNATIONAL RELATIONS OF A NEW TYPE

In a book published in 1964, two Soviet specialists in international relations analyze the "higher order" of transaction among system members and refer to it as a "new type of international relations."[1] Advancing a number of somewhat vague and unsystematic theories, the authors contend that, unlike the relationships among capitalist-imperialist states, profound qualitative advances are to be found in the relations among socialist nations, largely in the form of "brotherly mutual help, comradely cooperation, and firm and solid friendship among peoples who effectively manifest the principle of proletarian internationalism." As a further development, socialist internationalism is made an even more mature and progressive condition because of the formation of the socialist commonwealth of nations (sotsialisticheskoe sodruzhestvo narodov) comprising the international socialist system—the fourteen ruling-party states.[2] After a lengthy discourse on the origins and substance of these new relations, based upon the teachings of Marx, Engels, and Lenin, there follows an analysis of six categories of interaction; economic; political; ideological; cultural; international-legal; and finally, the influence of the socialist commonwealth upon contemporary international relations.

Of particular interest are the views on political cooperation, the exceptional essence of which is said to be a "cooperative dedication to Communist construction and its
eventual universal triumph." The broad political dedication uniting the commonwealth is basically twofold: (1) the
duty to facilitate the universal victory of communism "by
strengthening the world socialist system, the unity and
solidarity of its people, nations, and Marxist-Leninist parties, increasing its defensive might, and supporting all
workers who fight for freedom, national independence, and
socialism"; and (2) "political activity for the realization of
peaceful coexistence among countries with different social
systems—namely, the establishment of relations with capitalist, neutral, and newly independent governments."[3]

Directed toward these objectives, the foreign policies of
system members are characterized by: (1) political cooperation firmly based upon Marxism-Leninism with its objective
laws for both international and domestic development; (2)
maintenance of individual national independence and sovereignty; (3) sincerity and honesty (correspondence between
words and deeds), rooted in the power of socialism; (4)
solidarity of socialist countries, which serves the interests
of all peaceful peoples by restraining aggressive circles and
maintaining the forces for peace; and (5) recognition of the
Soviet Union's definitive role in the peace efforts of our
time.[4]

In brief, the foreign policy of the system is purportedly
not motivated by an arithmetical value—the increase in

membership since 1917—but rather by the substantive, scientifically-based efforts of fraternal socialist countries supported by their united economic, political, and military might. Most important are the authors' contentions that the most outstanding contributions to the foundation, affirmation, and development of socialist international relations have been made by such "authoritative Marxist leaders" as Dimitrov, Pieck, Zhivkov, Gomulka, Kadar, Ulbricht, Novotny, Tsedenbal (not East European, but Mongolian—and a member of COMECON nonetheless), and others.[5]

With reference to international agreements "founded upon fraternal friendship and cooperation," examples are drawn from East European members only—Rumania, Bulgaria, Hungary, and Czechoslovakia. Although it is stated that analogous comradely terminology can be found in agreements among other socialist states, none are mentioned. No mention is made of Mao Tse-tung, Ho Chi Minh, or any Asian Communist leaders. Interestingly enough, the emphasis throughout the book falls markedly upon the East European ruling-party leadership. The number of references to contemporary leaders ranges from five for Gomulka and Zhivkov, to three for Kadar and Novotny, and two for Ulbricht. Castro and Tsedenbal received five and two respectively. Yugoslavia and Albania are ignored, and, although Rumania continues to participate in COMECON and the Warsaw Pact and appears to be within the mainstream of ideologically permissible politics, references to its leadership are noticeably absent.

Looking ahead, the authors recall the Party program of

the 22nd Congress, its predictions for a "new type of international relations," and the inevitable transformation of
capitalism into communism. According to their description:

> Our era is correctly called the epoch of
> war between two opposed social systems,
> of socialist and national-liberational revo-
> lutions, the downfall of imperialism, the
> liquidation of colonialism, the transition
> to socialism by all peoples, and the triumph
> of socialism and communism on a world scale. [6]

Once directed toward these goals, and resting securely
upon Marxist-Leninist foundations, the foreign policies of
system members are *ipso facto* of a higher order. This in
Soviet theory is the essential rationale and meaning of "the
new type of international relations."

In the legal realm, integration and higher forms of international relations have reportedly already made such qualitative advancement that it is even possible to speak of "socialist
international law." One of the foremost legal experts of the
Soviet Union, Professor G. T. Tunkin, has attempted the following clarification:

> It is necessary to offer a definition of gen-
> eral international law and a separate de-
> scription of the socialist principles and
> norms operative in relationships among
> countries of the socialist camp . . . .
> This does not at all mean that we recog-
> nize the existence of a special international
> law governing the relationships among
> countries of the socialist camp and wholly
> excluding the operation of general inter-
> national law in these relationships. The
> proposal to which we refer derives from

> the fact of the existence of a number of
> socialist principles and norms that have
> come into being or are coming into being
> in relationships among countries of the
> world system of socialism, the specific
> nature of which cannot be encompassed
> in the general definition of international
> law. [7]

It is important to note that although Tunkin does not make the distinction between socialist international law and general international law clear, he is nevertheless attempting to make it. Airapetian and Sukhodeev strive to be more specific in their rendition but still founder on the crucial matter of practical and demonstrable differences. Instead, they argue steadfastly that the principles of international law among socialist countries and the principles of their international relations are really one and the same—i.e., brotherly friendship, comradely mutual help, national independence and sovereignty, complete equality and respect for territorial integrity, and noninterference in one another's internal affairs. Aside from the fact that these attitudes are hardly new,[8] why, one may ask, should they not prevail in the relations of, say, Poland or Czechoslovakia with nations of the world outside the international socialist system? Reduced to its most basic elements, the explanation lies in a strained logic purporting to show that the above principles apply only to states united by common Marxist-Leninist political institutions and objectives which receive concrete expression in the "peaceful labors" of WTO and COMECON—as contrasted with the "aggressive intentions" and "inequalities" inherent in analogous but inferior West European organizational efforts.[9]

As an interesting sidelight imparting a pedagogical dimension, the Soviet Institute of State and Law has several departments devoted to legal studies, among which are included a Department of International Law and a Department of International Law of a New Type (among socialist countries).[10] Even in the Marxist-Leninist purview, it should be clear that associations and organizational arrangements among socialist states are admittedly peculiar in that they do not readily lend themselves to study and analysis in terms of general international law which regulates relations between states and not parties. But of this, more needs to be said by Communist theoreticians themselves.

As mentioned earlier, on the theoretical level, the "new type of international relations" denotes two qualitatively different conditions. The more pristine and rudimentary (but widespread) is proletarian internationalism, signifying an aggregate of principles collectively guiding the world movement as a whole. In its contemporary form, the expression refers to a broad and highly inclusive alliance embracing four main sources of strength: (1) the fourteen ruling-party states; (2) all non-ruling Communist parties; (3) all parties and organizations united in the national liberation movement in developing nations; and (4) all peoples and organizations fighting against imperialism and for peace.[11] With specific reference to the most advanced member of the international socialist system:

> Proletarian internationalism is manifested
> in Communist construction in the Soviet
> Union. Working to build the first Communist

society in history, the CPSU and the entire
Soviet people are discharging their great
international duty and fulfilling Lenin's be-
hests—to do "the utmost possible in one
country <u>for</u> the development, support and
awakening of the revolution <u>in all</u> countries."
Ties of proletarian internationalism bind
the CPSU and all the Soviet people with the
fraternal parties and working people in all
countries. The Socialist Soviet state has
not and cannot have any interests in international affairs which would not correspond
to the deepest aspirations of all mankind. [12]

Socialist internationalism is a far more exclusive condition, applying to a "higher order" of relations among ruling-
party states only. As sovereign political entities and units in
a broad international community, [13] the ruling-party states
are constructing socialism, presumably on the Soviet model,
and are also deriving benefits from membership and cooperation in common economic, military, and cultural enterprises,
thereby enjoying multiple contributions to their individual
strengths, to that of the socialist system as a whole, to general
proletarian unity, and finally to individual foreign policies with
non-Marxist-Leninist states in the world at large. In this way
even the smallest increments of success at the more parochial
nation-state level bear multiple advances individually and collectively on each of <u>four</u> levels. The order of increasing so-
phistication and priority would be as follows: (1) general international relations as an all-encompassing activity; (2) proletarian internationalism; (3) socialist internationalism; and (4)
the East European subsystem with the Soviet Union at its
center.

The bedrock of socialist internationalism is said to rest upon the public order system prevailing in all fourteen Marxist-Leninist states. The abolition of private property and the public ownership of the means of production supposedly preclude the exploitation of man by man and simultaneously establish the essential conditions for a close fraternal association of peoples with a common purpose—i. e. , the eventual victory of socialism and communism in their countries. [14] Unity and strength are expressed in five principal ways—common ideology, aims, defense, identity, and interests: (1) Marxist-Leninist states are bound together by the common ideology of scientific Marxism-Leninism; (2) espousing common aims, they all strive for socialism and communism both at home and abroad; (3) they all steadfastly struggle against a common enemy, imperialism; (4) owing to their analogous political, economic, social, and cultural systems, they possess a common identity causing them to be more akin to each other than to any outsider; and (5) they have common short-range interests and experience joint accomplishments: namely the further development of socialism, communism, mutual economic and military assistance, and fraternal cooperation among all members. [15]

Departing from these official proletarian and socialist variants rendered by Soviet and East European theoreticians, "international relations of a new type" can really mean at least four different, if closely interrelated, things. At the practical level and emerging with Chairman Khrushchev's formulations in 1955, one rendition may be subsumed under

96

the rubric, "The Commonwealth of Socialist Nations," including the principles of non-aggression, non-intervention in domestic affairs, sovereign equality, and mutual assistance, all of which are said to provide the cement of unity among the fourteen ruling-party states. In effect, the Chairman's overriding emphasis upon state sovereignty and independence served to eclipse any definitive projections regarding relations among the parties themselves and, more importantly, any specific projections about the world movement as a whole. Receiving further emphasis at the 20th Party Congress in the dispensations regarding many roads to socialism, this tendency was dramatically reinforced by subsequent Polish and Hungarian bids for independence and the more successful machinations of the Chinese, whose deviation continues to serve as an alternative locus of system power. More recently, a prominent Soviet economist stated the position almost in the form of a summary bill of rights for smaller nations.

> International relations of a new type, which
> are being formed by world socialism, are
> based on the principle of self-determination,
> providing for the right of any nation--great
> or small--to form an independent state, and
> for completely voluntary decisions as to the
> nature and depth of relations with other so-
> cialist states. These relations most con-
> sistently express the principle of sovereignty
> which presupposes respect for the rights of
> every nation in the use of all its natural, eco-
> nomic and human resources within state fron-
> tiers. It means the incontestable right of each
> people to decide independently the fate of its
> own country.

Observance . . . of the principle of sovereignty demands non-intervention in each
other's internal affairs, mutual respect
for the laws and traditions of other countries, and the banning of acts aimed at
discrediting the party and state organs to
which a people has entrusted the government of its country. Non-intervention in
internal affairs presupposes the rejection
of the use of any means of economic, political or military pressure. Moreover, it
demands respect for territorial integrity
and historically formed state frontiers, and
excludes the non-peaceful settlement of any
territorial disputes.

Marxism-Leninism teaches that the socialist commonwealth can only be stable as a
voluntary union of equal independent states.
Any attempt artificially to accelerate, to
"push forward" the process of international-
ization, historical experience shows, leads
in the final analysis to the opposite result:
to an intensification of nationalism. Equality is incompatible with privileges for any
country, with attempts to impose the experience and methods of building socialism
in one country on other socialist countries.
It also implies strict reciprocity in cooperation. [16]

At this first level, then, the new type of international

relations is simply a function of polycentric communism with

sources and manifestations in the events analyzed in chapter

two dealing with the origins and dynamics of the international

socialist system. Thus, the new forms and degrees of re-

lations between the Soviet Union and the states of Eastern

Europe may be understood as a direct result of profoundly

disruptive changes within the system as a whole which neces-
sitated appropriate theoretical adjustments and explanations.
Rather than a guiding principle, socialist internationalism
and relations of a new type are essentially an inevitable consequence of realistic political intercourse, attendant upon
the unexpected and ideologically unaccounted-for dissolution
of a once monolithic empire. In practice, its distinguishing
characteristics include individual state sovereignty, limited
independence, national diversity, relaxation of tensions, and
a damper placed upon excessive Soviet intrusions in East
European affairs. Nationalism and particularism predomi-
nate.

Second, faced with the dynamics and flexibility of a
genuinely operative international system, likeminded Marxist-
Leninist states have promoted practical efforts at problem-
solving through functional international organization. The
most continuous and successful type of organizational activity
has understandably been in the area of joint economic planning with highly detailed and specific objectives. This activity goes on in a setting dominated by a commitment to indus-
trialize, accompanied by growing urbanization and a deepening
socioeconomic division of labor in each country and, more
recently, concerted efforts toward modernizing lagging economies in accordance with rational cost-price indices and
marketing techniques long prevalent in the West.

The record shows that political and economic integration
was least successful when the CPSU wielded a coercive monopoly over the process. The Stalin era saw minimum military

cooperation, little joint economic planning, few exchanges of information apart from an abject imitation of Soviet examples, and no important value-sharing among fellow Communist states. Integration was a one-way process in which the aims of the satellites were subordinated to those of the USSR. Once the rigidity of the bloc gave way in the fall of 1956, however, new trends emerged. Coercion yielded to a slow process of institutionalizing Soviet interests and voluntary exchanges based upon economic advantages and limited ideological compromise negotiated among "equals." In this sense, contemporary relations of a new type denote concrete organizational efforts which in their present setting are completely at variance with integrative policies of the Stalinist period. Based upon WTO and COMECON, the new focus is organizational, with wide institutional flexibility and multiple participation based upon national self-interest.

Third, from a theoretical point of view, international relations of a new type signify a historical era—a phase of development made possible by the establishment of a number of viable Marxist-Leninist states, socialist as yet, which in their current collective existence require authoritative doctrinal interpretation. Presently, there are no precise prognostications regarding the future status and characteristics of the nation-states or international relations under communism. Marx, Lenin, Stalin, and Khrushchev were notably silent or vague on these issues. Meanwhile, having evolved beyond socialism in one country (the USSR), Marxism-Leninism is today practiced in a system of diverse national

100

environments, experiencing an interim phase whose salient features are said to be of a higher, more perfect order, but necessarily prior to the ultimate condition—international communism. The emphasis in this third sense must be ideological and transitional—i. e., upon a traditionally predictable historical continuum and the system's current place in it.

Fourth, the new type of international relations is at its heart an admission that Marx and Lenin were wrong: worldwide communism is at best only a hope, and in order to preserve something of a time-weathered and beleagured ideological substructure, compromises and adjustments must be effected in the face of a markedly narrowed field for the realization of international communism on any level. In this connection, the central ideas of this study have attempted to cast light upon the implicit and explicit roles which the Soviet Union's East European allies are performing and, further, the interdependence which derives from what must be (or at least appears to be) a collective enterprise of concrete acts in the service of doctrinal retrenchment and eventual ideological fulfillment. Common experiences in reconstruction following World War II, together with the shared political origins of Eastern Europe's ruling-party states (again with the exception of Yugoslavia and Albania), are in this fourth sense conducive to preserving a pattern of associations. Included are habits of mind and vested interests collectively projecting an ethos distinguishing the East European subsystems and imparting a minimal unifying force of considerable longevity for all concerned.

Historically the British Commonwealth set a precedent for the transformation of empire into a peaceful association of widely disparate but equal nation-states. Communism sees the nation-state as obsolete and envisions its own commonwealth as a proletarian union of mankind on earth, without all the paraphernalia of national frontiers. The nation, however, continues to be a persistent feature in the present transitional phase, a factor which suggests that interim solutions must understandably include some kind of formalized interstate arrangements, uniting independent member governments in their Marxist-Leninist activities and aspirations. Indeed, it should not be surprising if, in the not too distant future, the character of international relations in Eastern Europe were to assume qualities similar to those evinced in the protracted evolution of the British Commonwealth. In this fourth sense, then, international relations of a new type can mean the incipient stages of a genuinely operational commonwealth of sovereign Marxist-Leninist states centered in Eastern Europe, possessing loose but deeply felt ties and gradually developing independent but acceptable positions on a number of international questions. The orientation is rational rather than doctrinaire, predominantly East European rather than systemwide, and, at the surface, highly productive of copious revolutionary verbalizations and ostentatious demonstrations of unity.

As a final point, Airapetian's and Sukhodeev's culminating contention appears to be that the eventual operational scope and significance of intra-system activity is virtually without limits:

> The world socialist system will become a
> great force which will not only determine
> the chief content, trend, and nature of
> historical development, but all of its trends,
> all paths of societal development, all inter-
> national events, the entire world situation,
> and the whole system of contemporary
> international relations. [17]

A more realistic stance would counsel caution. The
authors' zeal is understandably great, but their compass is
too wide. The international relations which they purport to
analyze are quite imperatively of a new type, especially when
it is understood that the ultimate fulfillment of the Soviet
political system, as it has been outlined for a half century, is
at stake. But barring the further expansion of communism in
which the USSR would stand pre-eminent (a quite unlikely
prospect), the Soviets must prove the viability of the pro-
verbial new relations not by relying upon the total international socialist system as presently fragmented—but rather
upon the only sector reasonably available to them. Due to the
dynamics of polycentrism, the geographical context for Airapetian's and Sukhodeev's sanguine predictions has been reduced considerably, a development to which the conspicuous
concentration of "the most authoritative Marxist leaders"
would seem to lend credence.

More than this, however, the challenge of peaceful coexistence aimed toward the force of example cuts both ways.
In the long run, the world's bystanders will not accept ideological cant for truth. If the multi-dimensional international
relations of a new type, or any type, are to determine the

world's future, much more evidence must be provided that Marxist-Leninist states—especially the favorably situated and endowed subsystem members of Eastern Europe—can really outdistance the West in self-declared targets. Compelling though the challenge must be, the Soviets must admit that competitive coexistence of different social systems means everything it says and that continued economic growth in the United States, its capitalist system and "culpable" policies notwithstanding, only belies the assertion that communism is more productive, efficient, historically superior, and therefore destined to dominate the world.

CONCLUSIONS

The Soviet Union has demonstrated two cardinal interests in its foreign policy toward Eastern Europe—the first
national, the second ideological. The first has always been
supreme in an international crisis, since without it the second would be defenseless and illusory. The second, however,
has never been consciously sacrificed for the first and has in
fact grown in scope and variety as the Communist bloc has
given way structurally to a system in which ideological commitment rather than overt coercion came to serve as the
irreducible unifying force. Meanwhile, an increase in the
number of adherents to Marxism-Lenism has, paradoxically,
encumbered efforts to promote proletarian internationalism
within the framework of doctrinal orthodoxy, and demonstrated that commitments tailored by national distinctions
can be tenuous and potentially unreliable.

The primary catalyst in this transformative process has
been nationalism, the age-old bogeyman of Marxism-Leninism
and of every other social theory dispensed for universal application. If nationalist sentiments have frequently been ex-
ploited for the goals of communism, they have also proved to
be highly detrimental to the sort of ideological unity and

proletarian consciousness which the Soviets have espoused
for years. The pattern of Communist security behavior has
unequivocally shown that difficult situations arise when leaders
place the national element first. Unmistakably, this was the
case with Stalin during World War II; with Tito in his heated
quarrel with the Kremlin; with Gomulka and Imre Nagy in their
protests against periodic Soviet intrusions; with Hoxha in his
fears of too intimate a rapprochement between Tito and the
Kremlin; and with Ceausescu and the late Gheorghiu-Dej in
their adamant dedication to economic and political self-
reliance.

Under the generic umbrella of "proletarian internationalism" there is presumed to be an all-encompassing community
of interests, uniting the world movement and radiating solidarity. But success in establishing a number of ruling-party
states since World War II, plus wide differences in stages of
economic development and deeply held national aspirations,
have rendered the overarching community of aims more questionable and subject to parochial interpretation—which is to
say, precisely the way the Soviet Union interpreted its own
interests following the Bolshevik Revolution. Granted that
no official renunciation of basic ideological tenets has taken
place; yet vacillation between a stress upon ingrained national
distinctions on the one hand, and universalistic Marxist-
Leninist premises on the other, has acted to weaken the binding nature of these premises for all national parties concerned. The dichotomy between Russian nationalism and
Soviet communism was itself starkly revealed during World

War II when the USSR was assisted not by appeals to Marxism-Leninism, but, among other things, by an awakening of Great Russian nationalism. Ironically enough, in proving the utility of this dependable force for defending the Soviet Union, the Kremlin unwittingly tested the usefulness of the very instrument which proved decisive in the debilitation of its monolithic bloc. There followed the development of an international system containing constellations of powers whose alignments reflected serious differences in matters of both domestic and international politics.

Overwhelming in their impact, these developments bear one predominant message: unity in the total international system is only an idea imbedded in the collective historical mind of the Communist movement. None of the important trends of the last decade would indicate that its accomplishment is ultimately possible.

The task in this study has been to confront this reality and suggest that a gradual relativization of ideological commitment has endangered the self-declared mission of the Soviet Union and has elevated the need to promote attractive projects in Eastern Europe reflecting more meaningful, if geographically limited, proletarian and socialist internationalism, plus Marxist-Leninist orthodoxy. While it may be argued that in theory, internationalism and doctrinal orthodoxy are mutually reinforcing, in practice, they have proved incompatible. This incompatability, however, has not deterred the USSR from treating the gamut of Eastern European developments as a fundamental national interest essential to the promotion of the Soviet political system beyond socialism in one country.

Historically strategic to the territorial defense of the USSR, Eastern Europe by the mid-50's had acquired greater significance in terms of at least four security-related priorities: (1) the ideological commitment to the successful expansion and fruition of Marxism-Leninism on an international plane; (2) elaborate programs for concerted political and economic integration designed to hasten "the simultaneous entry into communism within one and the same historical epoch" with, of course, appropriate allowances for the admittedly undefined character of this process; (3) the military pledge to regard any threat to a Warsaw Pact signatory a threat to the Soviet Union itself; and (4) the Soviet need to protect its great-power status based upon a social system rapidly maturing at home, but only in somewhat earlier stages in Eastern Europe.

As an ideologically oriented great power and the first Marxist-Leninist state, the USSR must ultimately depend upon its political transplants abroad. Gradual, if modest, developments, coupled with appropriate doctrinal interpretations, function to preserve the faith with all its exciting encomiums about a more or less simultaneous entry into communism and all the rest. Granted that this is a pretentious and visionary way of describing a commitment to the highest form of Marxist-Leninist relationships, as yet unrealized; the fact remains that it is precisely this vision that constitutes the underpinnings of an operational East European Communist subsystem with a unifying raison d'etre of its own.

One is reminded of a striking historical parallel harkening back to the Crusades of the Middle Ages. The orthodox development and future of Christian Europe was somehow perceived to depend upon freeing the holy places of the Near East from alien domination. Conversely, in the Soviet conception of the 20th century, the cradle of Marxism-Leninism is to be sustained by the great force of example and the eventual adherence of the earth's multitudes to the camp whose venerable doctrine proves most productive of success and protective of the enduring values of mankind, "properly understood." Soviet political elites have fixed the future of a deeply vested way of life on their ability not only to produce the abundance long awaited by the Soviet populace, but also to control and defend specially designated territory as a requisite to their own regime security and ultimate doctrinal verification.

Yet aside from these historical and theoretical considerations, there is a more immediate and practical need. Whatever else the conclaves of Communist parties in March 1965 and April 1967 proved, they demonstrated that, except for Rumania, the active East European Party states of COMECON and the Warsaw Pact were conspicuous among the delegations which journeyed to Moscow and Karlovy Vary for purposes of pondering unity. Although a number of these cautioned against rash gambits which would openly read the Chinese and their ideological cohorts out of the system, their presence was basically supportive of the Soviet stance as enunciated by the post-Khrushchev leadership. Indeed, with the exception of

Yugoslavia and Albania, all the ruling-party states of
Eastern Europe owe their political origins to the USSR; and
if they manage to fulfill the internationalist roles which Communist theoreticians have elaborated, they will in a prophetic
sense be helping to sustain the very originator and origins
of Marxism-Leninism itself. To say the least, from the
Soviet point of view, this would be a most important historical debt repaid. A number of geographical, historical, and
military factors can be cited to explain this unique interdependence. But the heightened significance of reliable support in the face of accelerated multi-polarity within the
international socialist system should not be overlooked:
since 1960, the competition and quarrels with China have
caused the USSR to place the highest premium upon endorse-
ment of its positions by its closest allies—meaning members
of COMECON and the Warsaw Pact. As at least a partial
return on an enormous political and ideological investment,
such support in times of stress cannot but highlight the advantages of the ''ever-growing cooperation and unity of the
countries comprising the socialist camp,'' or at least that
part within the perimeter of certain Soviet military controls.

Mutual dependence is by definition a two-way street, and
although the USSR remains dependent upon its former satellites in a number of respects, only the Soviets presently
possess the wherewithal essential for the rapid development
of intrasystem economies. Reduced to its simplest terms,
the practical interrelationship means, on the one hand,
Soviet dependence upon system-member behavior as at

least partial but last-resort confirmation for Marxist-Leninist writ, and on the other, the preference by "true" allies for contemporary Soviet formulas—peaceful coexistence, destalinization, and pragmatic adjustments to pressing realities—as necessary prerequisites for much-desired costly modernization and industrialization, supported by the Soviet Union's ample and impressive resources.

Perhaps all too tragically, these facts have borne down harshly upon the Chinese and Albanians who in Moscow's book have pursued reckless deviationist policies threatening to rend the system asunder. Repeated warnings have been voiced, punctuated by references to the indispensable advantages of fraternal cooperation and integration which unrepentant system deviates only forfeit by persistently recalcitrant stands. As a punitive consequence, they only deny themselves the benefits of Soviet economic largesse. More than this, persistent overtures to both the Chinese and Albanians have the gnawing effect of not only reminding them of their desperate need for Soviet economic aid, and, in the Chinese case, even diplomatic and military support, but also convey to potential dissenters the Soviet resolve to deal sternly with future cases—thus pointing out how costly factionalism and "splitism" can really be and how essential it is to promote the cohesion and further integration of the system rather than jeopardize its integrity. Clearly, the dictates of need have generated strong interdependence and its unavoidable corollary—reciprocal reliance.

Any case for Soviet-East European interdependence is palpably weakened by Rumania's independent gestures. [1] Once one of Moscow's most docile satellites, Rumania has since 1963 opposed Soviet projects for binding supernational planning and all forms of economic cooperation that might impinge upon national sovereignty. The chief issue has been its refusal to become a breadbasket and vegetable garden in the Balkans while other nations of Eastern Europe are left to develop their industrial capacities freely. The fact is that Bucharest has not been enthusiastic about many of COMECON's policies and tends to look upon its own economy as essentially a national responsibility to be spared outside interference and dictation. Harkening back to the summer of 1963, when Rumania had proceeded with her own industrialization campaign, the Party's Declaration of Independence (April 1964) expressed these objections unequivocally and forcefully. Among other things, the Declaration stressed the sovereign independence of all Communist parties, denounced any notion of "parent and son" relationships, and eschewed all attempts by one party to interfere in the affairs of another.

Regarding Sino-Soviet polemics, the Rumanians made headlines by publishing substantial fragments of the now-famous Chinese Letter to Moscow, June 16, 1963, in which embarrassing Sino-Soviet differences were aired. The Rumanian Party organ, Scinteia, was the only East European newspaper to report at length on Peking's letter which, along with a Soviet reply, was finally published by Pravda on July 14, 1963. In the main, the Rumanian position attempted to make

the best of both worlds: in the April 1964 Declaration, it
was strongly critical of China's irascible behavior and penchant for ideological bombast, and, while generally supportive of Soviet views, it suggested first that Moscow was
unnecessarily enthusiastic about forcing tensions to a head,
and second that no party should be ostracized from the system because of Soviet displeasure. The refusal in June 1966
to permit Chou En-lai a platform for the greater aggravation
of the Moscow-Peking split further demonstrated Bucharest's
resolve to pursue a middle course, a policy which seems likely
to continue.

This study makes no pretense of minimizing the significance of these developments or, indeed, the seriousness of
Rumania's absence from the solemn Moscow and Karlovy Vary
meetings, which probably had an unsettling effect upon Soviet
plans for disciplining China and perhaps other schemes for
restoring "normalcy" to the system as a whole. An extraordinary series of policies has likewise caused the Soviets to
be understandably uneasy and solicitous about relationships
heretofore taken for granted. Following the rupture in Soviet-
Albanian diplomatic relations in December 1961, and the
comprehensive withdrawal of East European diplomatic repre-
sentation from Tirana, the Rumanian Ambassador was re-
turned to his post in March 1963. Party leader Nicolai
Ceausescu, in a number of highly nationalistic speeches following the March 1965 conclave, strongly criticized Moscow's
past treatment of Rumania, and particularly underscored some
highly tendentious historical accounts of the Red Army's

wartime liberational role and postwar political engineering in Eastern Europe. He also unearthed sensitive questions regarding the postwar disposition of Bessarabia and demanded the abolition of such military blocs and alliances as NATO and the Warsaw Pact. Since then, limitations have been placed on the teaching of Russian in Rumanian schools at all levels, and the once influential Maxim Gorki Russian Language Institute has been closed. Finally, at least twice in two years, Rumania split with her East European colleagues in UN voting: the first time in November 1963, regarding a de-nuclearized zone in Latin America, and the second in November 1964, over the question of the non-proliferation of nuclear weapons.

As bold manifestations of national self-reliance, these moves certainly would seem to parry Soviet initiatives toward ideological retrenchment and the preservation of subsystem cohesion. Attracting the attention, if not amazement, of the world to what have been nothing short of brilliantly executed positions of independence within the system, they confirm beyond question the dogged persistence of nationalist preferences at variance with Communist publicity. Providing a veritable mine of rich material for diplomatic historians, the Rumanian record includes skillful timing and deft maneuvers in the maintenance of correct relations with China, Yugoslavia, Albania, and the more orthodox people's and socialist democracies—all this accompanied by some, although not irretrievable, deterioration in relations with the USSR, plus an impressive improvement in economic and cultural ties with the West.

114

Only a short decade ago, such a state of affairs would have been unthinkable. Today it is possible because of four major factors: (1) a tightly organized and unified Rumanian Communist Party which, in an uncommonly smooth transition from the Gheorghiu-Dej to the Ceausescu leadership in the spring of 1965, demonstrated its exceptional political integrity and cohesion; (2) the extraordinary potential for intrasystem maneuvers provided by Sino-Soviet competition and conflict; (3) the successful example of Yugoslavia, which provided an attractive model for all aspiring independents; and (4) the beginnings of what appears to be a more receptive, sensitive, and activist Western policy toward Eastern Europe. [2]

Granted the newsworthiness of these exceptional feats of independence, Rumania continues in her own national way to operate as a dedicated and relatively conservative Marxist-Leninist state within the framework of East European politics. This is also a meaningful focus for attention. What seems to be evident in the Soviet reaction is a tactful and cautious attitude that the Rumanians must not be pushed into reckless demonstrations of independence which the dynamics and logic of system developments have quite naturally allowed them. The problem for the Rumanians is not merely an independent stance or deviation from a Soviet position, but rather how far a deviation can really go without eliciting Soviet reprisals. The Chinese and Albanian cases tentatively show that the area of permissible conflict stops short of a tacit commitment to ideological fundamentals and the willingness to promote security, increased growth, and integration within the system. Marxist-Leninist states which go beyond this minimum automatically place themselves outside the pale of fraternal preference and support from Moscow—which is just what China and Albania have chosen to do.

The Rumanians for their part must keenly sense the limitations of nationalist bravado and the rational boundaries of their admittedly assertive stance. So far their political acumen and diplomatic agility have been superlative. One must always bear in mind that from the outside, dissidence within the system invariably appears to spell the doom of the movement, while to those inside, expressions of independence denote deep changes, to be sure, but a healthier political environment nonetheless, and a mode of operations much preferred to that of Stalin's day. The pattern of subsystem interaction is thereby complicated and volatile, thus necessitating genuine efforts toward mutual accommodation and increasingly sophisticated policies for balancing particularistic interests. Given the magnitude of commitments to greater questions, however, the Soviet leadership can only be challenged by centrifugal pressures and respond appropriately to reformulate and shore up what remains of the actual potential for Marxist-Leninist fulfillment.

Never before has the Soviet capacity for ingenuity and adaptation been under greater stress. If there is a dominant current in the decade initiated by the Polish and Hungarian uprisings in the fall of 1956, it is one of unsettling change. Reflect a moment on the developments. The beginnings of

the Khrushchev decade witnessed a stunning disintegration of
the Stalinist empire, followed by a protracted and painstaking
restoration of Soviet authority in Eastern Europe. Highlighting the fact that the expansion of world communism does not
necessarily accrue to the advantage of the USSR, a new phase
appeared in 1960-61 in which the effects of Chinese emergence
were manifested with great fanfare and tension. The long-
prevalent vision of a bifurcated Europe receded, and the
stark juxtaposition of blocs gave way to expanding opportunities for maneuver. Formerly impervious frontiers and rigid
demarcations between NATO and Warsaw Pact countries were
eroded by the dictates of national interest and the mutual advantages of trade. What was formerly monolithic revealed
schism, embarrassing ideological disputation, and the genuine workings of an international system in which the
heightened frequency of interaction among Marxist-Leninist
states signified the give-and-take of authentic international
politics. At least one rewarding by-product was the realization that as the Communist camp had increased in size, the
independence-maintaining properties of its units were im-
measurably enhanced. The resultant systemwide unknowns
and variables caused the Soviets to rely more closely upon the
governments and parties of Eastern Europe. Because they
could no longer command them in the old way, they had to
pay a price.

Herein lies one of the most engrossing paradoxes of contemporary Communist politics. On the one hand, the fourteen
Marxist-Leninist states comprise a viable international

system which has long dispensed with stringent Soviet tutelage and the Stalinist fetish for monolithism and homogene-
ity. Unmistakably, the trend has been toward reciprocal
accommodation without destroying the privileged position of
the USSR, which, by virtue of its lengthy headstart and overwhelming economic power, remains the strongest state of
all. Joined together by conventions, treaties, and sundry
agreements of a military, political, economic and cultural
character, the system (especially its East European grouping) has shown a marked urge toward increased organization
and institutionalized cooperation, bearing multiple options,
exchanges, compromises, and mutual benefits for member
states—in short, a highly complex pattern of international
behavior.

On the other hand, interparty relations have tended to
deteriorate in almost direct proportion to improvements at
the functional and governmental levels.[3] Soviet efforts to
bring dissident parties into line have largely failed, and the
schisms within the ideological substructure proceed apace,
thus requiring continuous doctrinal agility. Shaken by the
Titoist bolt in 1948 and barely weathering the Polish and
Hungarian ''Octobers'' of 1956, the Soviet Union experienced
a second round with Yugoslavia in 1958, the deviationist col-
lusions of the Chinese and Albanians (as contrasted wtih the
more conformist stance of the East Germans, Czechoslovaks,
and Bulgarians), and most recently the Rumanian overtures
for substantial individuality in matters of economic and foreign policy.

What continues to gather momentum is a trend whereby intrasystem party unity is increasingly compromised on behalf of regional integration based on a community of East European national interests rather than on dogmatic rectitude. By realistically accepting the possibility of limited ideological disagreement, both the Khrushchev and Brezhnev-Kosygin leaderships have attempted to paper over the problem of ideological purity. They have set their sights upon more feasible, if limited, objectives. Concessions were made, and are being made, to the centrifugal forces within the East European subsystem in order to strengthen its political, economic, and social foundations, and thus develop as a whole that section of the international system in which Soviet national interests and expectations are greatest. If Soviet leaders must advocate worldwide communism and dream about its mythological comforts, the most they may realistically expect is that carefully cultivated relationships with their East European neighbors might brighten the prospects for communism on a genuinely international, if disappointingly local, scale. (Certainly the confrontation with China has shelved the larger hope.) It would in any case be far easier to countenance socialism in one country if it were to proceed vigorously with the advancement of socialism in many countries: What better way to prepare for a more or less simultaneous transition to communism than the dedicated strengthening of its preceding and requisite phase all around? And at least a semblance of what Marx and Lenin regarded as inevitable is preserved in the bargain.

119

One need not accept a conspiracy theory of communism to understand that in Soviet-East European relations there lies potential stopgap vitality for the challenged leadership of the CPSU in the international socialist system. Given the need to resuscitate some of the old revolutionary zeal and sense of mission, multi-functional enterprises among the most "fraternal" system members can now help to generate a timely and indispensable motor force. Notwithstanding troublesome complications and setbacks, achievements arising from mutual cooperation would presumably demonstrate that, in the international sphere, Marxism-Leninism need not be relegated to the realm of dogmatic discourse or scattered guerrilla operations and wars of national liberation. Indeed, in the Soviet view, the East European area is the closest approximation of a going concern, the living unity of theory and practice, a showpiece and testimony to evolving socialist relationships on an international scale.

Thus constituting a less than perfect solution, this set of international relationships reminds one of an earlier Soviet experience in pragmatism. If Stalin's practical priority for "socialism in one country" was calculated to make of the USSR first an impregnable bastion and then a waystation to eventual worldwide programs, the construction of "socialism in many countries" can be viewed in the 60's as a necessary prerequisite for the realization of international communism, if only on a scale considerably smaller than Marx and Lenin envisioned. As a transitional phase, "regional socialism in one subsystem" performs a compromise function not unlike that performed by the building of "socialism in one country" for the USSR in the 20's and 30's. There need not be a pell-mell disintegration of a secular faith (the theme of Lowenthal's able study), if the Soviets can once again manage successful retrenchment. Of course the Stalinist priority was first and foremost for consolidating the Soviet Union's base of national power—that is, it was avowedly nationalist in emphasis. The contemporary emphasis shifts increasingly to the international arena, although to be sure, this shift bears compelling significance for the vitality and political influence of the original base itself.

At the 22nd Party Congress, Chairman Khrushchev declared that the former Dictatorship of the Working Class had become a Dictatorship of the Whole People, presumably signifying the end of all antagonisms and the inauguration of a new era of grandiose economic programs for the creation of abundance and a speedy transition to communism. More subtle was the inference that the motive force for revolutionary change had descended to the economic base where Marx had always said it rightly belonged. Admittedly, the superstructure of Party tutelage and planning was to continue, but the only genuine and peaceful proof of the Marxist-Leninist future was consigned to the realm of increased productivity and the accumulation of wealth.

> After all, goulash does not fall from
> heaven. In order to have abundant food
> and clothing, it is necessary to have
> highly developed productive forces.

> All blessings are created by human labor.
> The better and the more man works, the
> more wealth is created for society. [4]

Events since Khrushchev's replacement have indicated a
continuing policy to produce more of everything. But more
than this, the perceptible transformation of the CPSU from an
infallible elite directing an ideological revolution from above
to a party intimately dependent upon economic success is both
heretical and suggestive. Its portent is goulash socialism in
one country. And although the Soviet people would certainly
be receptive to such a development, it is imperative that the
utopian and internationalist goals of the future be continually
stressed and provided with persuasive meaning; otherwise,
the Party will appear to be making the efficiency and productivity of the present system an end in itself. Such a preference would not only run afoul of internationalist commitments, but also constitute anathema to the Kremlin leadership and its already beleaguered sources of authority.

The 23rd Party Congress, in March 1966, was hardly
eventful in generating sorely needed revolutionary inspira-
tion. [5] In the main it proved to be a striking confirmation of
the Brezhnev-Kosygin political style which, under the twin
lash of unabating polycentrism and pressing domestic programs, has demonstrated calm patience, restraint, and a
willingness for conciliation. In the international realm, this
has meant support for a loose-knit worldwide movement of
equal and autonomous parties, as distinct from a formal
international of the earlier model. A remarkably prosaic

gathering, productive of little more than bland restatements,
the 23rd Congress broached no new theories of international
relations and left participants with little more than the over-
lapping concepts of proletarian and socialist internationalism
which are already palpably frayed and probably untenable.
Sounding communism's familiar drumbeat, General Secretary
Brezhnev reiterated the Soviet Union's "unswerving loyalty
to its internationalist revolutionary duty and the tasks of
strengthening the solidarity of the commonwealth of socialist states." Repeatedly he referred to the world system of
socialism as "a tremendous historical victory of the international working class, the principal revolutionary force of
our epoch, and the most reliable bulwark of all peoples who
are fighting for peace, national freedom, democracy and
socialism."[6]

At the Ninth Congress of the Bulgarian Communist Party
in November 1966, the Soviet General Secretary continued the
theme:

> Lenin emphasized that the first duty of the
> Communist Party of each socialist country
> both to its own people and to working people
> throughout the world consists in carrying
> the socialist revolution to a conclusion in
> its own country and successfully building
> socialism and then communism. This is
> our international as well as our national
> duty.
>
> Following Lenin's behests and showing the
> world an example of international brother-
> hood and comradeship, the socialist coun-
> tries are successfully developing their

> cooperation on the basis of socialist inter-
> nationalism. The mutual relations of the
> socialist member states of the Warsaw Pact
> and the Council for Mutual Economic Aid
> provide a good example of such cooperation
> . . . . The concern . . . for further de-
> veloping political, economic and cultural
> cooperation among the socialist countries,
> for bringing their economies closer to-
> gether and for strengthening the WTO is
> persuasive testimony to its unshakable
> fidelity to the principles of socialist inter-
> nationalism.
>
> We are completely convinced that the unity
> of the international Communist movement
> and the solidarity of its militant detach-
> ments will steadily grow and become
> stronger. It is a joy to us all to acknowl-
> edge that today, as always, the Bulgarian
> Communist Party . . . marches in the
> ranks of the most active fighters for this
> unity and for the purity of our ideological
> weapons![7]

Even at the risk of overemphasis the Soviets continue to

aver that unity, if only in appearances, is vitally important.

As the trustees of the most mature sector of the system,

East European Party elites harbor at least a vestige of that

inexplicable sentiment which is bound to prevail—that is,

somehow the movement with which they have all identified so

long must be unified, lest continued symptoms of international

disunity eventually present insurmountable challenges to their

own oligarchic legitimacy. The East European leadership

need not be reminded that the alternative to a modicum of sub-

system harmony might well mean catastrophe for themselves,

and that by engaging in explosive actions and pressuring what
little remains of the system's most cohesive part, they only
render international Communist goals more illusory and
undermine the legitimacy of the CPSU and their own exclu-
sivist parties as well.

In the final analysis, only steady infusions of futuristic
planning, distributive gains (or welfare communism), seman-
tic revolution, and vigorous but mainly ritual internationalism can create momentum for Marxist-Leninist political
systems and bring them within reach of long-professed goals.
There is no ready formula for this problem. A great deal
depends upon the ability of the Soviet leadership to respond
with deft and timely mixtures of both cautious pragmatism
and ideological fundamentalism. Balanced judgment would
seem to suggest that the Brezhnev-Kosygin tandem is already
forging ahead with what appears to be the dexterity of accomplished political empiricism. But the plain truth is that,
whatever its commendable achievements to date, the Soviet
Union cannot remain revolutionary if its accomplishments
lag and the predictions upon which its future depends fail to
materialize. The continued pressure of failure is likely to
cause the CPSU to perform the functions of a traditional
political party whether it likes it or not. Meanwhile, given
the plausibility of a more or less simultaneous entry into
communism by a select group of East European states—the
full definition of the phrase "simultaneous entry" to be
wisely held in abeyance—the Soviet leadership can ease its
own and the Party's transformation by acting to breathe

new life into the revolutionary mythology and Marxist-Leninist mystique which have served it so well.

RECAPITULATION

The chief arguments in this study have been as follows.

1.   Marxism-Leninism is an inextricable part of political legitimization in the USSR, and the Communist Party's claimed exclusive possession of it is its only genuine source of authority.

2.   According to Communist theoreticians, Marxism-Leninism is a doctrine which finds its ultimate fulfillment in an international context only.

3.   The attainment of socialism in one country (in fact four countries—USSR, Czechoslovakia, Rumania, and Yugoslavia) means that for the Soviets, the future of communism must be continually sustained by events abroad. As presently constructed, Soviet doctrine does not posit the feasibility of communism in one country.

4.   For historical, geographical, and political reasons, Eastern Europe is the only international context amenable to ideological confirmation on behalf of the USSR, a situation which is somewhat paradoxical in that, faced with system-wide conflicts, the Soviets must ultimately rely upon their East European allies, among whom national particularism

began in the first place. As an important consequence, the old one-way relations have been replaced by an operational and loosely institutionalized subsystem harboring an atmosphere of mutual dependence and value-sharing.

5. There is thus an important qualitative difference between Soviet-East European relations and those within the rest of the system, largely because Soviet interaction with East European states bears an inherent theoretical content and built-in proposition which underpins the Soviet political system itself. These relations also have an exceptional internationalist purpose, unlike the relations of, say, the United States and its allies, which seem to have no other objective except peace and harmony. Finally, the Soviet Union, although vastly superior in power, is intimately dependent upon its own political transplants abroad and not necessarily upon states dedicated to Marxism-Leninism but with an indigenous Communist heritage and power base.

6. The geographical history of communism shows that revolutionary initiatives have shifted from Marx's industrialized proletarian Europe to Lenin's agrarian Russia—the weakest link in the worldwide capitalist chain—and now finally, according to Mao Tse-tung, to the village populations of Asia. But if Mao points to Asia as the vigorous new repository of "truth" and ultimate success, the Soviet leadership can point to Eastern Europe (hardly rural in Mao's terms) as the most mature and sophisticated collective effort on behalf of international communism to date.

7.   Although the USSR cannot expect to realize worldwide communism as it has been consistently envisioned, perhaps international communism might be accomplished on a narrower, more local scale. The impossibility of reconciling communism in one country with existing doctrine need not prevent concerted Soviet efforts toward establishing communism in one bloc or subsystem, a goal which is at least plausible and perhaps attainable, but by no means inevitable.

8.   Lastly, is the title of Airapetian's and Sukhodeev's book far off target? Never before has the self-projected maturation and fruition of a political system depended so heavily upon international relations and external events. Regardless of whether international relations of a new type signify polycentric communism, a doctrinaire historical phase, organizational cooperation, or a developing commonwealth of loosely associated sovereign states, the CPSU faces the most far-reaching challenge and responsibility of its history: for the future of the Soviet political process as we know it, and of communism as a political ideology with universal application, may well depend upon the outcome of precisely all these new relations among the subsystem nations of Eastern Europe.

APPENDIX I

TREATY OF FRIENDSHIP, COOPERATION, AND MUTUAL
ASSISTANCE BETWEEN THE PEOPLE'S REPUBLIC OF BUL-
GARIA, THE HUNGARIAN PEOPLE'S REPUBLIC, THE GER-
MAN DEMOCRATIC REPUBLIC, THE POLISH PEOPLE'S
REPUBLIC, THE RUMANIAN PEOPLE'S REPUBLIC, THE
UNION OF SOVIET SOCIALIST REPUBLICS, AND THE
CZECHOSLOVAK REPUBLIC.
SIGNED AT WARSAW ON 14 MAY, 1955 (entered into force,
June 6, 1955).*

The Contracting Parties,
Reaffirming their desire to create a system of collective security in Europe based on the participation of all
European States, irrespective of their social and political
structure, whereby the said States may be enabled to com-
bine their efforts in the interests of ensuring peace in
Europe;
Taking into consideration, at the same time, the situation
that has come about in Europe as a result of the ratification of
the Paris Agreements, which provide for the constitution of a
new military group in the form of a "West European Union,"
with the participation of a remilitarized West Germany and its

---

*United Nations Treaty Series, Vol. 219, No. 2962 (1955).
The German Democratic Republic actually adhered to the Treaty
in January 1956, after establishing the National People's Army
and Ministry of Defense.

inclusion in the North Atlantic bloc, thereby increasing the danger of a new war and creating a threat to the national security of peace-loving States;

Being convinced that in these circumstances the peace-loving States of Europe must take the necessary steps to safeguard their security and to promote the maintenance of peace in Europe;

Being guided by the purposes and principles of the Charter of the United Nations;

In the interests of the further strengthening and development of friendship, cooperation, and mutual assistance in accordance with the principles of respect for the independence and sovereignty of States and of nonintervention in their domestic affairs;

Have resolved to conclude the present Treaty of Friendship, Cooperation, and Mutual Assistance and . . . have agreed as follows:

Article 1. The Contracting Parties undertake, in accordance with the Charter of the United Nations, to refrain in their international relations from the threat or use of force and to settle their international disputes by peaceful means in such a manner that international peace and security are not endangere

Article 2. The Contracting Parties declare that they are prepared to participate, in a spirit of sincere cooperation, in all international action for ensuring international peace and securi and will devote their full efforts to the realization of these aim

In this connection, the Contracting Parties shall endeavor to secure, in agreement with other States desiring to cooperate in this manner, the adoption of effective measures for the general reduction of armaments and the prohibition of atomic, hydrogen, and other weapons of mass destruction.

Article 3. The Contracting Parties shall consult together on all important international questions involving their common interests, with a view to strengthening international peace and security.

Whenever any one of the Contracting Parties considers that a threat of armed attack on one or more of the States Parties to the Treaty has arisen, they shall consult together immediately with a view to providing for their joint defense and maintaining peace and security.

Article 4.   In the event of an armed attack in Europe on one
or more of the States Parties to the Treaty by any State or
group of States, each State Party to the Treaty shall, in the
exercise of the right of individual or collective self-defense,
in accordance with Article 51 of the United Nations Charter,
afford the State or States so attacked immediate assistance,
individually and in agreement with the other States Parties
to the Treaty, by all the means it considers necessary, including the use of armed force.   The States Parties to the
Treaty shall consult together immediately concerning the
joint measures necessary to restore and maintain international peace and security.

Measures taken under this article shall be reported to
the Security Council in accordance with the provisions of the
United Nations Charter.   These measures shall be discon-
tinued as soon as the Security Council takes the necessary
action to restore and maintain international peace and
security.

Article 5.   The Contracting Parties have agreed to establish
a Unified Command, to which certain elements of their armed
forces shall be allocated by agreement between the Parties,
and which shall act in accordance with jointly established
principles.   The Parties shall likewise take such other concerted action as may be necessary to reinforce their defensive strength, in order to defend the peaceful labor of their
peoples, guarantee the inviolability of their frontiers and
territories, and afford protection against possible aggression.

Article 6.   For the purpose of carrying out the consultations
provided for in the present Treaty between the States Parties
thereto, and for the consideration of matters arising in connection with the application of the present Treaty, a Political
Consultative Committee shall be established, in which each
State Party to the Treaty shall be represented by a member
of the Government or by some other specially appointed
representative.

The Committee may establish such auxiliary organs as
may prove to be necessary.

Article 7.   The Contracting Parties undertake not to participate in any coalitions or alliances, and not to conclude any
agreements, the purposes of which are incompatible with the
purposes of the present Treaty.

The Contracting Parties declare that their obligations under international treaties at present in force are not incompatible with the provisions of the present Treaty.

Article 8. The Contracting Parties declare that they will act in a spirit of friendship and cooperation to promote the further development and strengthening of the economic and cultural ties among them, in accordance with the principles of respect for each other's independence and sovereignty and of nonintervention in each other's domestic affairs.

Article 9. The present Treaty shall be open for accession by other States, irrespective of their social and political structure, which express their readiness, by participating in the present Treaty, to help in combining the efforts of the peace-loving States to ensure the peace and security of the peoples. Such accessions shall come into effect with the consent of the States Parties to the Treaty after the instruments of accession have been deposited with the Government of the Polish People's Republic.

Article 10. The present Treaty shall be subject to ratification, and the instruments of ratification shall be deposited with the Government of the Polish People's Republic.

The Treaty shall come in force on the date of deposit of the last instrument of ratification. The Government of the Polish People's Republic shall inform the other State Parties to the Treaty of the deposit of each instrument of ratification.

Article 11. The present Treaty shall remain in force for twenty years. For Contracting Parties which do not, one year before the expiration of that term, give notice of termination of the Treaty to the Government of the Polish People's Republic, the Treaty shall remain in force for a further ten years.

In the event of the establishment of a system of collective security in Europe and the conclusion for that purpose of a General European Treaty concerning collective security, a goal which the contracting Parties shall steadfastly strive to achieve, the present Treaty shall cease to have effect as from the date on which the General European Treaty comes into force.

Done at Warsaw, this fourteenth day of May, nineteen hundred fifty-five, in one copy, in the Russian, Polish, Czech, and German languages, all the texts being equally authentic. Certified copies of the present Treaty shall be transmitted by the Government of the Polish People's Republic to all the other Parties to the Treaty.

IN FAITH WHEREOF the Plenipotentiaries have signed the present Treaty and have thereto affixed their seals.

By authorization of the Presidium of the National Assembly of the People's Republic of Albania:
(Signed) M. Shehu

By authorization of the Presidium of the National Assembly of the People's Republic of Bulgaria:
(Signed) V. Chervenkov

By authorization of the Presidium of the Hungarian People's Republic:
(Signed) A. Hegedüs

By authorization of the President of the German Democratic Republic:
(Signed) O. Grotewohl

By authorization of the Council of State of the Polish People's Republic:
(Signed) J. Cyrankiewicz

By authorization of the Presidium of the Grand National Assembly of the Romanian People's Republic:
(Signed) G. Gheorghiu Dej

By authorization of the Presidium of the Supreme Soviet of the Union of Soviet Socialist Republics:
(Signed) N. Bulganin

By authorization of the President of the Czechoslovak Republic:
(Signed) V. Široký

APPENDIX II

CHARTER OF THE COUNCIL FOR MUTUAL ECONOMIC
ASSISTANCE. SIGNED AT SOFIA, ON 14 DECEMBER
1959 (entered into force April 13, 1960)*

The Governments of the People's Republic of Albania,
the People's Republic of Bulgaria, the Hungarian People's
Republic, the German Democratic Republic, the Polish
People's Republic, the Romanian People's Republic, the
Union of Soviet Socialist Republics and the Czechoslovak
Republic,

BEARING IN MIND that the economic co-operation which
is successfully taking place between their countries helps to
promote the most rational development of the national economy,
to raise the level of living of the people and to strengthen the
unity and solidarity of those countries;
    DETERMINED to continue the development of comprehen-
sive economic co-operation based on consistent implementation
of the international socialist division of labour in the interests
of the building of socialism and communism in their countries
and the maintenance of lasting peace throughout the world;
    CONVINCED that the development of economic co-operation
between their countries contributes to the achievement of the
purposes set forth in the Charter of the United Nations;

---

*United Nations Treaty Series, Vol. 368, No. 5245 (1960).

AFFIRMING their readiness to develop economic relations with all countries, irrespective of their social and political structure, on the basis of equality, mutual advantage and non-intervention in each other's domestic affairs;

RECOGNIZING the increasing importance of the part played by the Council for Mutual Economic Assistance in the organizing of economic co-operation between their countries,

HAVE AGREED, to these ends, to adopt the present Charter.

Article I

PURPOSES AND PRINCIPLES

1. The purpose of the Council for Mutual Economic Assistance is to promote, by uniting and co-ordinating the efforts of the member countries of the Council, the planned development of the national economies and the acceleration of the economic and technical progress of those countries, the raising of the level of industrialization of the countries with a less-developed industry, and a continual growth in the productivity, together with a steady increase in the well-being of the peoples, of the member countries of the Council.

2. The Council for Mutual Economic Assistance is based on the principle of the sovereign equality of all the member countries of the Council.

Economic and scientific-technical co-operation between the member countries of the Council shall take place in accordance with the principles of complete equality of rights, respect for sovereignty and national interest, mutual advantage and friendly mutual aid.

Article II

MEMBERSHIP

1.   The original members of the Council for Mutual Economic Assistance shall be the countries which have signed and ratified the present Charter.

2.   Membership in the Council shall be open to other European countries which subscribe to the purposes and principles of the Council and declare that they agree to accept the obligations contained in the present Charter.

New members shall be admitted by a decision of the Session of the Council, on the basis of official requests by countries for their admission to membership in the Council.

3.   Any member country of the Council may leave the Council, after notifying the depositary of the present Charter to that effect.   Such notice shall take effect six months after its receipt by the depositary.   Upon receiving such notice, the depositary shall inform the member countries of the Council thereof.

4.   The member countries of the Council agree:
(a)   To ensure implementation of the recommendations, accepted by them, of organs of the Council;
(b)   To render to the Council and its officers the necessary assistance in the execution of the duties laid upon them by the present Charter;
(c)   To make available to the Council the material and information essential to the fulfillment of the tasks entrusted to it;
(d)   To keep the Council informed of progress in the implementation of the recommendations adopted in the Council.

Article III

FUNCTIONS AND POWERS

1. In conformity with the purposes and principles set forth in article I of the present Charter, the Council for Mutual Economic Assistance shall:

(a) Organize:
Comprehensive economic and scientific-technical co-operation among the member countries of the Council, with a view to the most rational use of their natural resources and the more rapid development of their productive forces;

The preparation of recommendations on the most important questions in the economic relations resulting from the plans for the development of the national economies of the member countries of the Council, for the purpose of co-ordinating those plans;

The study of economic problems which are of interest to the member countries of the Council;

(b) Assist the member countries of the Council in the preparation and execution of joint measures regarding:

The development of industry and agriculture in the member countries of the Council, based on consistent implementation of the international socialist division of labour and on specialization and co-operation in production;

The development of transport, for the primary purpose of ensuring the conveyance of the increasing volume of export-import and transit freight between member countries of the Council;

The most effective use of the capital invested by member countries of the Council in projects to be carried out on the basis of joint participation;

The development of the exchange of goods and services between member countries of the Council and with other countries;

The exchange of experience in the matter of scientific-technical achievements and advanced methods of production;

(c) Undertake other action required for achieving the purposes of the Council.

2.   The Council for Mutual Economic Assistance,
through its organs acting within their competence, is authorized to adopt recommendations and decisions in accordance
with the present Charter.

Article IV

RECOMMENDATIONS AND DECISIONS

1.   Recommendations shall be adopted on questions of
economic and scientific-technical co-operation. Such recommendations shall be communicated to the member countries
of the Council for consideration.

Recommendations adopted by member countries of the
Council shall be implemented by them through decisions of
the Governments or competent authorities of those countries,
in conformity with their laws.

2.   Decisions shall be adopted on organizational and pro-
cedural questions. Such decisions shall take effect, unless
it is specified otherwise in them, from the date on which the
record of the meeting of the Council organ concerned is signed.

3.   All recommendations and decisions of the Council
shall be adopted only with the consent of the member countries
concerned, each country being entitled to state its interest in
any question under consideration by the Council.

Recommendations and decisions shall not apply to countries which state that they have no interest in the question at
issue. Nevertheless, each such country may subsequently
associate itself with the recommendations and decisions
adopted by the remaining member countries of the Council.

Article V

ORGANS

1.   For the discharge of the functions and the exercise of
the powers mentioned in article III of the present Charter, the
Council for Mutual Economic Assistance shall have the following
principal organs:

The Session of the Council,
The Conference of representatives of the countries in
  the Council,
The Standing Commissions,
The Secretariat.

2.   Other organs may be established, as necessary, in
conformity with the present Charter.

Article VI

THE SESSION OF THE COUNCIL

1.   The Session of the Council shall be the highest organ
of the Council for Mutual Economic Assistance. It shall be
authorized to discuss all questions falling within the competence of the Council, and to adopt recommendations and decisions in accordance with the present Charter.

2.   The Session of the Council shall consist of delegations from all the member countries of the Council. The
composition of the delegation of each country shall be determined by the Government of the country concerned.

3.   The regular sessions of the Council shall be convened twice a year in the capital of each member country of
the Council in turn, under the chairmanship of the head of the
delegation of the country in which the session is held.

4.   A special session of the Council may be convened at
the request or with the consent of not less than one third of
the member countries of the Council.

5.   The Session of the Council shall:

(a) Consider:
Proposals on questions of economic and scientific-
technical co-operation submitted by member countries of
the Council, as well as by the Conference of representatives
of the countries in the Council, the Standing Commissions
and the Secretariat of the Council;

141

The report of the Secretariat of the Council on the activity of the Council;

(b)   Determine the course of action of the other organs of the Council, and the main questions for the agenda of the next session of the Council;

(c)   Perform such other functions as may be found necessary for achieving the purposes of the Council.

6.   The Session of the Council is authorized to establish such organs as it may consider necessary for the discharge of the functions entrusted to the Council.

7.   The Session of the Council shall establish its own rules of procedure.

Article VII

THE CONFERENCE OF REPRESENTATIVES
OF THE COUNTRIES IN THE COUNCIL

1.   The Conference of representatives of the countries in the Council for Mutual Economic Assistance shall consist of representatives of all member countries of the Council, one for each country.

The representative of a country in the Council shall have, at the headquarters of the Secretariat of the Council, a deputy together with the necessary number of advisers and other staff. The deputy, when so authorized by the representative, shall perform the functions of representative in the Conference.

2.   The Conference shall hold its meetings as necessary.

3.   Within its field of competence, the Conference shall have the right to adopt recommendations and decisions in conformity with the present Charter.   The Conference may also submit proposals for consideration by the Session of the Council.

4.   The Conference shall:

(a) Consider proposals from the member countries of the Council, the Standing Commissions and the Secretariat of the Council regarding the implementation of the recommendations and decisions of the Session of the Council, as well as other questions connected with economic and scientific-technical co-operation which need to be settled in the period between sessions of the Council;

(b) Engage in preliminary discussion, where necessary, of the proposals made by member countries of the Council, by the Standing Commissions and by the Secretariat of the Council regarding items for the agenda of the next session of the Council;

(c) Co-ordinate the work of the Standing Commissions of the Council, and study their reports on the work completed and on future activities;

(d) Approve:
The personnel and budget of the Secretariat of the Council, and the report of the Secretariat on the operation of the budget;
The regulations for the Standing Commissions and Secretariat of the Council;

(e) Establish control organs for supervising the financial activity of the Secretariat of the Council;

(f) Perform other functions arising from the present Charter and from the recommendations and decisions of the Session of the Council.

5. The Conference may set up auxiliary organs for preparatory work in regard to items of the agenda.

6. The Conference shall establish its own rules of procedure.

Article VIII

THE STANDING COMMISSIONS

1. Standing Commissions of the Council for Mutual Economic Assistance shall be set up by the Session of the Council

for the purpose of promoting the further development of economic relations between the member countries of the Council and organizing comprehensive economic and scientific-technical co-operation in the various sectors of the national economies of those countries.

The regulations for the Standing Commissions shall be approved by the Conference of representatives of the countries in the Council.

2.   Each member country of the Council shall appoint its representatives to the Standing Commissions.

3.   The Standing Commissions shall have the right, within their field of competence, to adopt recommendations and decisions in conformity with the present Charter. The Commissions may also submit proposals for consideration by the Session of the Council and the Conference of representatives of the countries in the Council.

4.   The Standing Commissions shall work out measures and prepare proposals for implementing the economic and scientific-technical co-operation mentioned in paragraph 1 of this article; they shall also perform other functions arising from the present Charter and from the recommendations and decisions of the Session of the Council and of the Conference of representatives of the countries in the Council.

The Standing Commissions shall submit to the Conference of representatives of the countries in the Council annual reports on the work done and on their future activities.

5.   The meetings of the Standing Commissions shall, as a rule, be held at their permanent headquarters, which shall be designated by the session of the Council.

6.   The Standing Commissions may establish auxiliary organs, as necessary. The composition and terms of reference of such organs, and their place of meeting, shall be determined by the Commissions.

7.   Each Standing Commission shall have a Secretariat, headed by the Secretary of the Commission. The establishment

pertaining to the Secretariat of a Commission shall be a part of the Secretariat of the Council and shall be maintained from the budget of the Council.

8.   The Standing Commissions shall establish their own rules of precedure.

Article IX

THE SECRETARIAT

1.   The Secretariat of the Council for Mutual Economic Assistance shall consist of the Secretary of the Council, his deputies and such personnel as may be required for the performance of the functions entrusted to the Secretariat.

The Secretary and his deputies shall be appointed by the Session of the Council and shall direct the work of the Secretariat of the Council.   The personnel of the Secretariat shall be recruited from citizens of the member countries of the Council, in accordance with the regulations for the Secretariat of the Council.

The Secretary of the Council shall be the chief officer of the Council.   He shall represent the Council vis-à-vis officials and organizations of the member countries of the Council and other countries, and vis-à-vis international organizations. The Secretary of the Council may authorize his deputies, as well as other members of the Secretariat to act on his behalf.

The Secretary and his deputies may take part in all meetings of the organs of the Council.

2.   The Secretariat of the Council shall:

(a)   Submit a report on the Council's activity to the regular Session of the Council;

(b)   Assist in the preparation and conduct of meetings of the Session of the Council, the Conference of representatives of the countries in the Council and the Standing Commissions of the Council, and of meetings convened by decision of those organs of the Council;

(c)   Prepare, when so instructed by the Session of the Council or by the Conference of representatives of the countries in the Council, economic surveys and studies on the basis of material submitted by member countries of the Council, and publish material on questions regarding economic and scientific-technical co-operation between those countries;

(d) Prepare:

Proposals concerning the work of the Council, for consideration in the appropriate organs of the Council;

Information and guidance on questions involved in economic and scientific-technical co-operation between member countries of the Council;

(e) Organize, jointly with the Standing Commissions of the Council, the preparation of draft multilateral agreements on questions arising from economic and scientific-technical co-operation, on the basis of recommendations and decisions adopted by the Session of the Council and by the Conference of representatives of the countries in the Council;

(f) Undertake other action arising out of the present Charter, the recommendations and decisions adopted in the Council, and the regulations for the Secretariat of the Council.

3. The Secretary of the Council, his deputies and the personnel of the Secretariat, when fulfilling the duties entrusted to them, act as international officials.

4. The headquarters of the Secretariat of the Council shall be in Moscow.

Article X

PARTICIPATION OF OTHER COUNTRIES IN
THE WORK OF THE COUNCIL

The Council for Mutual Economic Assistance may invite countries which are not members of the Council to take part in the work of the organs of the Council.

The conditions under which the representatives of such countries may participate in the work of the organs of the Council shall be determined by the Council in agreement with the countries concerned.

Article XI

RELATIONS WITH INTERNATIONAL ORGANIZATIONS

The Council for Mutual Economic Assistance may establish and maintain relations with the economic organizations of the United Nations and with other international organizations.

The nature and form of such relations shall be determined by the Council in agreement with the international organizations concerned.

Article XII

FINANCIAL QUESTIONS

1. The member countries of the Council for Mutual Economic Assistance shall bear the cost of maintaining the Secretariat and of financing its activity. The share of this cost falling to each member country shall be determined by the Session of the Council. Other financial questions shall be dealt with by the Conference of representatives of the countries in the Council.

2. The Secretariat of the Council shall submit to the Conference of representatives of the countries in the Council a report on the operation of the budget for each calendar year.

3. The maintenance expenses of participants in the meetings of the Session of the Council, The Conference of representatives of the countries in the Council and the Standing Commissions of the Council, and in all meetings held within the framework of the Council, shall be borne by the country sending its representatives to those meetings.

4. The expenses involved in the servicing of the meetings mentioned in paragraph 3 of this article shall be borne by the country in which those meetings are held.

Article XIII

MISCELLANEOUS PROVISIONS

1.   The Council for Mutual Economic Assistance shall enjoy, on the territories of all member countries of the Council, the legal capacity essential to the performance of its functions and the achievement of its purposes.

2.   The Council, as also the representatives of the member countries of the Council and the officers of the Council, shall enjoy, on the territory of each of those countries, the privileges and immunities which are necessary for the performance of the functions and the achievements of the purposes set forth in the present Charter.

3.   The legal capacity, privileges and immunities mentioned in this article shall be defined in a special Convention.

4.   The provisions of the present Charter shall not affect the rights and obligations of the member countries of the Council arising out of their membership of other international organizations, or out of international treaties which they have concluded.

Article XIV

LANGUAGES

The official languages of the Council for Mutual Economic Assistance shall be the languages of all the member countries of the Council.

The working language of the Council shall be Russian.

Article XV

RATIFICATION AND ENTRY
INTO FORCE OF THE CHARTER

1.   The present Charter shall be ratified by the signatory countries, in accordance with their constitutional procedure.

2.   The instruments of ratification shall be deposited with the depositary of the present Charter.

3.   The present Charter shall enter into force immediately after the deposit of instruments of ratification by all countries which have signed the Charter, and the depositary shall notify those countries thereof.

4.   With respect to each country which in accordance with article II, paragraph 2, is admitted to membership in the Council for Mutual Economic Assistance and which ratifies the Charter, this Charter shall enter into force from the date of the deposit by such country of its instrument of ratification of the Charter, and the depositary shall notify the other member countries of the Council thereof.

Article XVI

PROCEDURE FOR AMENDMENT OF THE CHARTER

Each member country of the Council for Mutual Economic Assistance may make proposals for the amendment of the present Charter.

Amendments to the Charter, when approved by the Session of the Council, shall come into force immediately after the ratifications of those amendments have been deposited with the depositary by all member countries of the Council.

Article XVII

FINAL PROVISIONS

This Charter has been drawn up in a single copy, in the Russian language. It shall be deposited with the Government of the Union of Soviet Socialist Republics, which shall send certified true copies of the Charter to the Governments of all the other member countries of the Council and shall notify those Governments, and the Secretary of the Council, of the deposit of the instruments of ratification with the Government of the USSR.

IN WITNESS WHEREOF the representatives of the Governments of the member countries of the Council for Mutual Economic Assistance have signed the present Charter.

DONE at Sofia, on 14 December 1959.

For the Government of the People's Republic of Albania:
A. Kellezi
For the Government of the People's Republic of Bulgaria:
R. Damyanov
For the Government of the Hungarian People's Republic:
A. Apro
For the Government of the German Democratic Republic:
B. Leuschner
For the Government of the Polish People's Republic:
P. Jaroszewicz
For the Government of the Romanian People's Republic:
A. Birladeanu
For the Government of the Union of Soviet Socialist Republics:
A. Kosygin
For the Government of the Czechoslovak Republic:
O. Šimunek

NOTES

Introduction

1. V. Israelyan, "Communist Construction in the Soviet Union and the Leninist Foreign Policy," International Affairs, No. 5 (May 1966), 6. Israelyan is Vice Chairman of the Scientific Council on Problems of the History of Soviet Foreign Policy and International Relations, Academy of Sciences of the USSR.

The International Socialist System

1. The Soviets employ the terms "world socialist system" and "international socialist system" when referring collectively to fourteen nations, all in some stage of self-declared Marxist-Leninist development and ruled by Communist parties. Included among the fourteen ruling-party states are the USSR, China, Poland, Czechoslovakia, East Germany, Rumania, Hungary, Bulgaria, North Korea, North Vietnam, Albania, Mongolia, Cuba, and Yugoslavia. The latter two were included among the "socialist countries" in the Pravda editorial, "For Marxist-Leninist Unity of the Communist Movement, For Solidarity of the Countries of Socialism," February 10, 1963.

The classic American study on the interrelationships among these nations is George Modelski, The Communist International System (Princeton, N.J.: Center for International Studies, 1961). See also Z. K. Brzezinski, The Soviet Bloc: Unity and Conflict (Cambridge, Mass.: Harvard University Press, 1960); Richard Lowenthal,

World Communism: The Disintegration of a Secular Faith
(New York: Oxford University Press, 1964); N. S. Khrush-
chev, Vital Questions of the Development of the Socialist
World System (Moscow: Foreign Languages Publishing
House, 1962), and Socialism and Communism (Moscow:
Foreign Languages Publishing House, 1963), chap. II; and
O. V. Kuusinen, et al., The Fundamentals of Marxism-
Leninism (Moscow: Foreign Languages Publishing House,
1963), chap. XXV. For current research, see a number
of perceptive studies by Jan F. Triska and Associates,
Stanford Studies of the Communist System, Stanford
University.

2.   Pravda, December 6, 1960, p. 4.

Eastern Europe--Core and Subsystem

1.   The East European grouping includes the USSR, Poland,
     Czechoslovakia, East Germany, Hungary, Rumania, and
     Bulgaria. As always, Yugoslavia and Albania pose spe-
     cial problems. For purposes of this study, Yugoslavia
     is considered an exceptional part of the international
     socialist system; however, it has never signed the Moscow
     Statement of November 21, 1960, and is not yet con-
     sidered a full member which takes active part in Eastern
     Europe's integrative activities or contributes to its major
     theoretical journals. The news that Albania was out of
     the Warsaw Pact as of January 1962 was reported by
     Radio Moscow on August 30, 1963. (East Europe, Oc-
     tober 1963, p. 38.) That Albania has not participated
     in the work of COMECON since the end of 1961, with-
     drew its representative from the Secretariat, and
     ceased paying dues was reported on Radio East Berlin,
     December 22, 1962. (East Europe, February 1963,
     p. 33.) Albania was invited to the January 1965 meet-
     ing of the WTO Consultative Council Meeting in Warsaw
     but refused to attend. The invitation suggests that, con-
     trary to some reports, Albania is technically still a
     member of the Warsaw Pact.

2.   On the subject of the entry into communism, see G. F.
     Achminov, ''Theoretical Problems of Communism and

the Twenty-first Party Congress," Bulletin: Institute for the Study of the USSR, VI, No. 3 (March 1959), and Program of the Communist Party of the Soviet Union, adopted by the 22nd Congress of the CPSU, October 31, 1961 (New York: Crosscurrents Press, 1961), Section VI.

3. N. S. Khrushchev, The International Situation and Soviet Foreign Policy, report given at the Third Session of the USSR Supreme Soviet on October 31, 1959 (New York: Crosscurrents Press, 1960); also, U.S. Congress, Senate, Khrushchev and the Balance of World Power, 87th Cong., 1st Sess., July 27, 1961, Doc. No. 66. For a convenient compilation of many of Chairman Khrushchev's statements on this subject, see U.S. Congress, Senate, Khrushchev on the Shifting Balance of World Forces, 86th Cong., 1st Sess., September 14, 1959, Doc. No. 57.

4. Khrushchev, Vital Questions of the Development of the Socialist World System, p. 13. The same material appeared in the World Marxist Review, September 1962, and in Kommunist, August 1962.

Communism--An International Doctrine

1. Program of the Communist Party of the Soviet Union, 22nd Congress, October 31, 1961, p. 23. For the thesis that communism as a social doctrine is international and cannot be conceived otherwise, see Kommunist, No. 1 (January 1957), 9. For more recent expressions of this, see the World Marxist Review and International Affairs, passim.

2. V. Granov, "Soviet Foreign Policy and the Historical Objective of the Working-Class Movement," International Affairs, No. 3 (March 1966), 18 (italics added).

3. Sidney I. Ploss, The Soviet Leadership Between Cold War and Detente (Philadelphia: University of Pennsylvania, Foreign Policy Research Institute, September 28,

1964); Soviet Politics Since the Fall of Khrushchev
(Philadelphia: University of Pennsylvania, Foreign
Policy Research Institute, January 15, 1965); Con-
flict and Decision-Making in Soviet Russia (Princeton:
Princeton University Press, 1965).

4.   Kuusinen, et al. , The Fundamentals of Marxism-
     Leninism, p. 625 (italics added).

5.   "For Marxist-Leninist Unity of the Communist Move-
     ment, for Solidarity of the Countries of Socialism,"
     Pravda, February 10, 1963.

6.   Fundamentals of Marxism-Leninism, p. 18.

7.   Kommunist, November 1964, pp. 54-55.

8.   Richard Lowenthal, "Schism Among the Faithful,"
     Problems of Communism, XI, No. 2 (January-Feb-
     ruary 1962), 14.

9.   Todor Zhivkov, "Unity of the Socialist Countries Is
     Decisive in Building Communism," World Marxist
     Review, VI, No. 1 (January 1963), 4-5.

10. "The Internationalist Duty of the Communists of All
     Countries," Pravda, November 28, 1965

11. Zbigniew Brzezinski and Samuel P. Huntington,
     Political Power: USA/USSR (New York: Viking Press,
     1965), pp. 69-70.

12. Khrushchev, Vital Questions of the Development of the
     Socialist World System, pp. 7, 45.

13. "For New Victories in the World Communist Movement,"
     Kommunist, No. 1 (January 1961), 16.

14. Ibid. , p. 34.

15. N. S. Khrushchev, "Speech in Budapest During Soviet
     Party and Government Delegation Visit," April 7, 1958
     Pravda, April 8, 1958.

16. N. S. Khrushchev, "Speech at Meeting of Csepel Iron and Steel Works During Stay in Hungary of Soviet Party and Government Delegation," April 9, 1958, in For Victory in Peaceful Competition With Capitalism (New York: E. P. Dutton and Co., 1960), p. 327. Since Khrushchev's ouster in October 1964, considerable speculation has centered on possible new directions or even substantive revisions in Soviet policy toward Eastern Europe. Although Khrushchev was officially criticized for numerous errors and shortcomings, there is as yet no hard evidence that either the theoretical or practical commitments to a "more or less simultaneous entry into communism" have been officially abandoned. Such a decision, of course, would signal the end of the international socialist system as presently constituted.

The Role of East European International Organizations

1. A useful select bibliography includes Z. K. Brzezinski, "The Organization of the Communist Camp," World Politics, XIII, No. 2 (January 1961); Robert S. Jaster, "CEMA's Influence on Soviet Policies in Eastern Europe," World Politics, XIV, No. 3 (April 1962); Ralph W. Johnson, "The Danube Since 1948," Year Book of World Affairs (London: Stevens and Sons, 1963); Andrzej Korbonski, "COMECON," International Conciliation, No. 549 (September 1964); Kazimierz Grzybowski, The Socialist Commonwealth of Nations: Organizations and Institutions (New Haven: Yale University Press, 1964); David D. Finley, "A Political Perspective of Economic Relations in the Communist Camp," Western Political Quarterly, XVII, No. 2 (June 1964).

2. Program of the Communist Party of the Soviet Union, 22nd Congress, October 31, 1961, p. 134 (italics original).

3. Technically speaking, as of the 1959 Sofia Convention, the Danube Commission, organized in August 1948 to promote technical cooperation in navigational matters,

ceased to be a separate international organization and became an integral part of COMECON. See Grzybowski, p. 143. Accurate information regarding the three systemwide organizations is always in very short supply. No effort is made here to evaluate the organizational activity and degree and frequency of participation by specific members, especially by the Asian ruling-party states.

4. Appendix I, Article VII. Note, however, that the alliance is open to any nation, regardless of social or political structure (Article IX). Members include the USSR, Poland, East Germany, Czechoslovakia, Hungary, Rumania, Bulgaria, and Albania (inactive). Non-East European ruling-party states are entitled to send observers to WTO activities and have on occasion done so.

5. There are abundant Soviet references to these matters: The Soviet Stand on Disarmament (New York: Crosscurrents Press, 1962), passim; N. Polyanov, "Time Will Not Wait," Izvestia, August 21, 1962, p. 2; and Yu. Frantsev, "Lessons on Munich," [references to "Bonn militarists" who are zealously trying to revive the old line], Pravda, December 29, 1962, p. 6. See especially N. S. Khrushchev, Speech at the 6th Congress of the Socialist Unity Party of Germany, Berlin, January 16, 1963 (New York: Crosscurrents Press, 1963), pp. 16-17; and Victor Mayensky, "Old Wheeze in a New Key," Pravda, June 19, 1966, p. 5.

6. A. A. Grechko, "The Patriotic and International Duty of the USSR Armed Forces," Krasnaya Zvezda, October 6, 1961, p. 2.

7. See Appendix I, Article 4.

8. Izvestia, March 14, 1957.

9. Pravda, December 18, 1956.

10. _Izvestia_, April 17 and May 28, 1957. In May 1958, the Soviet Government announced that it would withdraw its troops from Rumania. The agreements with Poland, Hungary, and East Germany are as of this writing still in force.

11. For coverage of these proposals at the Pact's "Summit Conference" in Bucharest, July 1966, see _Christian Science Monitor_, July 8, 9, and 11, 1966.

12. B. Miroshnichenko, "Socialist Internationalism and Soviet Foreign Policy," _International Affairs_, No. 3 (March 1966), 8.

13. "For New Victories in the World Communist Movement," _Kommunist_, No. 1 (January 1961), 15.

14. See Appendix II for text of the Charter. It should be noted that the organization did not have a formal charter until 1959.

15. This message from Moscow to Belgrade is quoted by Stefan Stolte, "COMECON in Search of New Members," _Bulletin: Institute for the Study of the USSR_, VII, No. 2 (February 1960), 34.

16. The ideological implications of these commitments had been given earlier expression when the Soviet Union in 1947 refused to permit Czechoslovakia's sharing in the benefits of the Marshall Plan. Writing in 1954, Max Beloff stated that "the Soviet refusal . . . was understandable if one accepted the fact that the economies of those countries (Poland and Czechoslovakia) would be replanned to suit the needs of a wider economic system of which they only formed a part, and which could not, therefore, allow for the new set of influences which acceptance of American aid would entail." "Problems of International Government," _The Year Book of World Affairs_ (London: Stevens and Sons, 1954), p. 12.

17. *The Road to Communism: Documents of the 22nd Congress of the CPSU*, October 31, 1961 (Moscow: Foreign Languages Publishing House, 1961), pp. 18-19.

18. Khrushchev, *Vital Questions of the Development of the Socialist World System*, pp. 19-20.

19. Abundant references to these special projects can be found in both *Pravda* and *Izvestia*, and especially in *Vneshnaia Torgovlia* and *International Affairs* (Moscow).

20. TASS, October 23, 1963. Cited by *East Europe*, December 1963.

21. *Christian Science Monitor*, June 15, 1966, p. 2; also A. Babadzhian and A. Nikitin, "International Bank for Economic Cooperation," *Vneshnaia Torgovlia*, No. 1 (January 1967), 15.

22. For a useful and comprehensive analysis of the Council's problems, see Egon Neuberger, *Soviet Bloc Economic Integration: Some Suggested Explanations For Slow Progress* (Santa Monica, Calif.: The RAND Corporation, RM-3629-PR, July 1963). The following were held to be the greatest obstacles to economic integration among system members in Eastern Europe: (1) the attempt by each East European country to protect its national sovereignty; (2) the existence of strong vested interests in each country in the form of nationalized industries; (3) the need to take positive actions in planned economies in order to achieve integration rather than relying merely on the removal of artificial barriers; (4) the very great differences in the levels of economic development of the various member countries; (5) the desire for autarky; (6) the absence of economic tools necessary for achieving a rational division of labor; and (7) the ideological preference for heavy industry in each country. For a Soviet view of some of these same problems, see B. Miroshnichenko, "Contemporary Problems of Economic Cooperation Among COMECON Members," *Voprosy Ekonomiki*, No. 9 (September 1963), 16-28.

23. "Economic Integration: Problems and Prospects,"
 Problems of Communism, VIII, No. 4 (July-August
 1959), 23-29.

24. Alfred Zauberman, "The CMEA: A Progress Report,"
 Problems of Communism, IX, No. 4 (July-August 1960),
 58.

25. John Pinder, "EEC and COMECON," *Survey*, No. 58
 (January 1966), 104.

26. *Pravda*, March 27, 1959.

27. Zhivkov, "Unity of the Socialist Countries Is Decisive
 in Building Communism," *loc. cit.*, p. 6 (italics in
 original).

28. N. S. Khrushchev, "Fidelity to Marxism-Leninism Is
 the Source of Great Victories" (statement in Budapest),
 Pravda, April 4, 1964.

29. M. S. Suslov, "The Struggle of the CPSU for the Unity
 of the World Communist Movement" (speech at the plenary meeting of the CPSU Central Committee, February
 14, 1964), *Pravda*, April 3, 1964.

30. E. Bugayev, "Marxism-Leninism and the International
 Unity and Solidarity of the Communist Parties,"
 Partiinaya Zhizn', No. 7 (April 1965), 52-53.

31. L. I. Brezhnev, "The Peoples of the Soviet Union and
 Czechoslovakia Have the Same Goals, A Common Des-
 tiny, A Common Future," *Pravda*, September 15, 1965.

32. D. S. Polyansky, "Forty-Eighth Anniversary of the
 Great October Socialist Revolution," *Pravda*, November 7, 1965.

33. Raymond L. Garthoff, "The Military Establishment,"
 East Europe, XIV, No. 9 (September 1965), 14.

34. See the report on WTO's meeting in Bucharest, <u>Chris-tian Science Monitor</u>, July 8, 1966.

35. A selective sampling from Soviet periodical literature such as <u>International Affairs</u> and <u>Kommunist</u>: "Collaboration and Mutual Aid -- An Important Factor in the Development of Productive Forces of the Countries of Socialism," "The Mighty Force of Fraternal Unity," "On a Firm Foundation," "Strengthening of Cooperation Is the Path to New Successes," "Work Out Problems of Cooperation of Socialist Countries More Profoundly," "Important Factor in the Development of Cooperation," "In An Atmosphere of Brotherhood and Mutual Understanding."

36. "The Supreme Internationalist Duty of a Socialist Country," <u>Pravda</u>, October 27, 1965.

International Relations of a New Type

1. M. E. Airapetian and V. V. Sukhodeev, <u>Novyi tip mezhdunarodnykh otnoshenii</u> (Moscow, 1964), p. 71.

2. The term "commonwealth" is an appropriate translation for the Russian <u>sodruzhestvo</u>, a concept first enunciated in October 1956. See Kurt L. London, "The Socialist Commonwealth of Nations: Pattern for World Communist Organization," <u>Orbis</u>, III, No. 4 (Winter, 1960). For a comprehensive analysis of proletarian and socialist internationalism, see Jan F. Triska, <u>The Socialist World in Search of a Theory</u>, Stanford Studies of the Communist System, Research Paper No. 8 (November 1965).

3. Airapetian and Sukhodeev, pp. 155-56.

4. <u>Ibid.</u>, pp. 157-58.

5. <u>Ibid.</u>, p. 152.

6. <u>Ibid.</u>, p. 13.

7. G. I. Tunkin, "The 22nd Congress of the CPSU and the Tasks of the Soviet Science of International Law," Sovetskoe Gosudarstvo i Pravo, No. 5, 1962. Cited in Soviet Law and Government, I, No. 3 (Winter, 1962-63), 25.

8. They were expressed at the Bandung Conference, April-May 1955, projected as a basis for Asian coexistence (Panch Shila), and later enunciated at the 20th Congress of the CPSU in February 1956.

9. Airapetian and Sukhodeev, pp. 223-41.

10. Gordon Skilling, "In Search of Political Science in the USSR," The Canadian Journal of Economics and Political Science, XXIX, No. 4 (November 1963), 519.

11. Boris N. Ponomaryev, "Proletarian Internationalism Is the Revolutionary Banner of Our Epoch," Pravda, September 29, 1964.

12. B. Miroshnichenko, "Socialist Internationalism and Soviet Foreign Policy," International Affairs, No. 5 (May 1966), 7.

13. I. Dudinsky, "A Community of Equal and Sovereign Nations," International Affairs, No. 11 (November 1964), 4.

14. S. Sanakoyev, "The Basis of the Relations Between the Socialist Countries," International Affairs, No. 7 (July 1958), 161.

15. Miroshnichenko, pp. 7-11; Airapetian and Sukhodeev, pp. 63-77; D. E. Mel'nikov and D. G. Tomashevskii (eds.), Mezhdunarodnye otnosheniia posle Vtoroi Mirovoi Voiny (International Relations After the Second World War), Vol. III (Moscow, 1965), pp. 136-141; and Program of the Communist Party of the Soviet Union, 22nd Congress, p. 25.

16. O. Bogomolov, "Basic Principles of the International Division of Labor," Voprosy Ekonomiki, No. 11 (November 1966), 111-12 (all italics original).

17. P. 263 (italics added).

Conclusions

1. Only the most salient of these can be mentioned here. For a fuller account, see especially J. F. Brown, "Rumania Steps Out of Line," Survey, No. 49 (October 1963), 19-34; R. L. Braham, "Rumania: Onto the Separate Path," Problems of Communism, XII, No. 3 (May-June 1964), 2-9; and J. F. Brown, The New Eastern Europe: The Khrushchev Era and After (New York: Praeger, 1966), pp. 64-71, 167-69, 174-76.

2. Brown, The New Eastern Europe..., p. 168.

3. Jan Triska, "Conflict and Integration in the Communist Bloc: A Review," Journal of Conflict Resolution, V, No. 4 (December 1961), 422.

4. N. S. Khrushchev, "Cordial Meetings, Fraternal Handshakes" (statement during Party and Government delegation visit in Budapest), Pravda, April 3, 1964.

5. In view of continued Sino-Soviet tensions, the statement that may well prove to be the most memorable was made by Janos Kadar, First Secretary of the Hungarian Socialist Workers' Party: "The Hungarian Communists are of the opinion that the touchstone of internationalism has always been and still is a consistent and comradely attitude toward the Soviet Union. There has never been, is not, and never will be, anti-Soviet Communism." "The 23rd Congress of the CPSU and Problems of International Relations," International Affairs, No. 5 (May 1966), 6.

6. Pravda, March 30, 1966.

7. Pravda, November 16, 1966.

SELECT BIBLIOGRAPHY

Airapetian, M. E. and Sukhodeev, V. V. Novyi tip mezh-dunarodynykh otnoshenii. Moscow, 1964.

Aspaturian, Vernon V. "Soviet Foreign Policy," in R. C. Macridis (ed.), Foreign Policy in World Politics. 2d. ed. Englewood Cliffs, N. J.: Prentice-Hall, 1962.

Brown, J. F. The New Eastern Europe. New York: Praeger, 1966.

Brzezinski, Z. K. The Soviet Bloc: Unity and Conflict. 2d. ed. New York: Praeger, 1962.

Dallin, Alexander, et al. (eds.). Diversity in International Communism. New York: Columbia University Press, 1963.

Fischer-Galati, Stephen (ed.). Eastern Europe in the Sixties. New York: Praeger, 1963.

Grzybowski, Kazimierz. The Socialist Commonwealth of Nations: Organizations and Institutions. New Haven: Yale University Press, 1964.

Kaser, Michael. COMECON: Integration Problems of the Planned Economies. London: Oxford University Press, 1965.

Kertesz, Stephen D. (ed.). East Central Europe and the World: Developments in the Post-Stalin Era. Notre Dame, Ind.: University of Notre Dame Press, 1962.

Korbonski, Andrzej. "COMECON," International Conciliation, No. 549. New York: Carnegie Endowment for
International Peace, 1964.

Kuusinen, O. V., et al. The Fundamentals of Marxism-
Leninism. Moscow: Foreign Languages Publishing
House, 1963.

Laqueur, Walter and Labedz, Leopold (eds.). Polycentrism. New York: Praeger, 1962.

————. "The End of the Monolith: World Communism in
1962," Foreign Affairs, XXXX, No. 3, April 1962.

Lowenthal, Richard. World Communism: Disintegration
of a Secular Faith. New York: Oxford University
Press, 1964.

Mackintosh, J. M. Strategy and Tactics of Soviet Foreign
Policy. New York: Oxford University Press, 1963.

Modelski, George. The Communist International System.
Princeton: Center of International Studies, December 1,
1960.

Morris, Bernard S. International Communism and American
Policy. New York: Atherton Press, 1966.

Peterson, William (ed.). The Realities of World Communism.
Englewood Cliffs, N.J.: Prentice-Hall, 1963.

Rubinstein, Alvin Z. The Foreign Policy of the Soviet Union.
New York: Random House, 1966.

Shoup, Paul. "Communism, Nationalism and the Growth of
the Communist Community of Nations After World War II,"
American Political Science Review, LVI, No. 4, December 1962.

Shulman, Marshall D. Stalin's Foreign Policy Reappraised.
Cambridge: Harvard University Press, 1963.

Skilling, H. Gordon. Communism—National and International:
Eastern Europe After Stalin. Toronto: University of
Toronto Press, in association with the Canadian Institute
of International Affairs, 1964.

Triska, Jan F. The World Communist System. Stanford:
Stanford Studies of the Communist System, 1964.

Ulam, Adam. The New Face of Soviet Totalitarianism.
Cambridge: Harvard University Press, 1963.

Zagoria, Donald S. The Sino-Soviet Conflict: 1956-1961.
Princeton: Princeton University Press, 1962.